ABOUT THE AUTHOR

Paul Mooney is Managing Director of Paul Mooney Associates. The company specialises in integrating corporate strategy and human resources. Established in 1991, it is now part of an elite, networked group of innovative consulting companies.

Paul began his working life as a craftsman in Dublin, subsequently moving into production management. He then worked with General Electric (GE) in a number of Human Resource positions prior to joining Sterling Drug as Personnel Manager – Ireland. Eventually, as Human Resource Director for Asia, he had responsibility for all personnel activity in the dynamic economies of the Far East.

Paul holds the National Diploma in Industrial Relations from the National College of Industrial Relations, a Post-Graduate Diploma and a Ph.D from Trinity College, Dublin. He is the author of one other book and numerous business booklets/articles on a range of Human Resource topics.

GH00363571

DEVELOPING THE HIGH PERFORMANCE ORGANISATION

BEST PRACTICE FOR MANAGERS

Paul Mooney

Oak Tree Press
Dublin

Oak Tree Press
Merrion Building
Lower Merrion Street
Dublin 2, Ireland

© 1996 Paul Mooney
Paperback edition 1998

A catalogue record of this book
is available from the British Library

ISBN 1-86076-088-0 Paperback
ISBN 1-86076-019-8 Hardback

Design by Q Design
Design Implementation by The Look and The Language
Printed in Ireland by Colour Books Ltd

Man finds no challenge in mediocrity.

Professor Jun Borremeo
Asian Institute of Management

DEDICATION

To all those who daily seek to improve organisation performance and the quality of organisation life.

ACKNOWLEDGEMENTS

Dr. Gerry Lyons and Dr. Eddie Molloy provided background information on several of the theoretical constructs addressed in this book and Eddie co-wrote the chapter on Structure. Client companies allowed me to explore the concepts — working in the "real world" helped reshape my thinking on the principles that provide high performance options to organisations.

Tom O'Driscoll and Niamh Imbusch worked through the early drafts on Performance Management and suggested many useful changes. Annette Cunniffe put the final package together. In addition to implementing the basic design concept, Jim MacCormaic also devoted much-appreciated time and energy to incorporating subsequent amendments. David Givens steered the project through with an abundance of patience and great attention to detail.

To each of the above, a sincere thanks and the usual absolution of responsibility for errors.

CONTENTS

PERFORMANCE PLANNING

PREFACE

This book has primarily been written to help practising managers cope with information overload. Volumes of material have been written on each of the topics addressed; the individual chapters are an attempt to distil the wisdom from the current literature and the best operating practices which we have seen in client companies. For practising managers who do not have the time or the inclination to conduct primary research, this book provides relatively easy access to leading edge ideas.

The book also reflects our internal philisophy of continuous improvement. Working with clients allows us to continually test and modify our understanding of organisation effectiveness. Distilling this experience into sets of operating principles and working models improves our effectiveness as a consulting group.

If you have any comments on this particular book or suggestions on additional topics you would like to see addressed in the future, please contact us.

PMA Consultants
7 Blackheath Court
Clontarf, Dublin 3

Phone: +353-1-833 0897
Facsimile: +353-1-833 5079

MISSION, VISION & VALUES

1.1 INTRODUCTION

▶ FROM SCEPTICISM TO "BORN AGAIN": THE DISCOVERY OF MISSION, VISION AND VALUES

Mention the terms Mission, Vision or Values and the eyes of most managers are likely to glaze over. These are not terms in everyday usage. On first exposure, the concepts often seem vague and somewhat "military". For people who have not been directly involved in working with these concepts, the impact of Mission, Vision and Values statements on organisations is often not clear and the response is sometimes one of confusion and cynicism.

From a personal initial stance of scepticism, this author has moved 180 degrees to becoming an avid supporter of these concepts because of their tremendous potential impact on organisational performance. While the establishment of a clear Mission, Vision or Values is not a panacea for all organisational ills (what is?) they often help to explain the "missing link" in the attainment of a highly competent, committed and productive workforce.

This section attempts to explain these concepts and to highlight their positive impact on organisational performance. Before we define the individual terms, it is important to understand the collective value of these concepts — the notion of organisational alignment.

ORGANISATIONAL ALIGNMENT

The key benefit of defining a company's Mission, Vision and Values revolves around the notion of organisational coherence or "alignment". Simply stated, if the various elements of an organisation are "aligned", this creates a strong "fit" between a company's strategy (business direction) and its culture (the way things are done within the company, its systems, policies, procedures, etc.). Good alignment helps an organisation to move forward along a defined path. Poor alignment dissipates energy and makes forward movement extremely difficult. (See Figure 1.)

FIGURE 1
Organisational Alignment

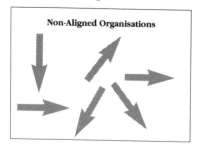

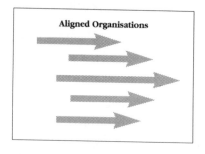

We must indeed all hang together, or most assuredly, we shall all hang separately

Benjamin Franklin

For any organisation the development of a clear Mission, Vision and Values (and the detailed action plans which support these) provides strategic focus which in turn guides business decisions and individual actions. This single focus also helps to overcome internal stakeholder rivalries (for example, between different departments) and releases internal energy where people become "committed" to a noble goal. It provides a graphic picture of a possible future state — and the organisation begins to move towards this. The concept of Mission thus applies equally well to all organisations whether private or public sector, commercial or voluntary.

ORGANISATIONAL ALIGNMENT: THE STRATEGIC FOCUS PLAN

Being good is not good enough when you dream of being great

Anon

In what may be called a Strategic Focus Plan, many companies are now fusing their business strategy and the supporting implementation plans into a single document. In a survey in the UK, 66 per cent of the companies surveyed had a defined Mission statement and linked strategic objectives (Klemm et al, 1989) with this statement. While this may not be a representative group (it is doubtful if such a high percentage of companies generally have fully developed these concepts), it highlights a definite world-wide trend towards the formal documentation of these concepts (Fulmer, 1992).

A Strategic Focus Plan which embraces Mission, Vision, Values and the supporting implementation plans is a combination of business strategy, philosophy and ethics. It is both a "hearts and minds" document which addresses the organisational need for intellectual rigor (what business are we in, where do we want to be in that business?) coupled with the need for an emotional message which recognises the human needs of organisation members.

A Strategic Focus Plan has six main elements: Mission, Vision, Values, Key Result Areas, Action Plans and Measurements. Each of these has a particular role to play in organisational performance:

1 **Mission** Provides "focus" by driving strategy. The absence of focus leads to dissipation of scarce resources. It answers the question "what business are we in?"

2 **Vision** Provides impetus through establishing targets and meaning. Vision creates or unleashes

"energy" by setting a noble goal which people strive towards. It answers the question "what is our short-term target?"

3 **Values** Provide control by guiding execution. Values are a roadmap in decision-making. They also create a sense for members that the organisation "stands for something". It answers the question "how do we want to behave?"

4 **Key Result Areas** These provide planning opportunity by breaking the total strategy into discrete "critical success factors". It answers the question "what are the areas which are critically important to succeed in?"

5 **Action Plans** These convert the "strategic intent" of the Mission, Vision and Values into concrete action plans with defined responsibilities and timings. It answers the question "what do I need to do on Monday next?"

6 **Measurements** These provide concrete milestones against which progress towards the company's Mission can be measured. It answers the dual questions "how will my/our performance be evaluated" and "how are we doing?"

WHAT IS ORGANISATION MISSION?

If you don't know where you are going you will probably end up somewhere else

Dr. David Campbell

Organisation mission describes the "present" purpose/non-purpose of the organisation. Its key benefit is to provide organisational focus and avoid dissipation of resources. It applies equally well to all organisations whether private or public sector, commercial or voluntary.

The absence of a considered mission outlining what business a company is in, its objectives and main criteria for measuring success (aside from the obvious profit motive) leaves an uncomfortable vacuum. El-Namaki (1992) described mission as "an explicitly identified domain/arena for combat" which captures the point well.

The concept of organisation mission first emerged in the early 1970s in Peter Drucker's notion of a "clear organisational mandate". Management beliefs about their mandate or charter, expressed in a mission statement, provide a guide for resource allocation decisions and also build a sense of unique corporate identity. For large geographically dispersed organisations, it provides a common direction that should transcend individual or specific location needs. To a lesser extent, it also has a public relations function in communicating a public image to important external stakeholders. While in practice, mission statements can be simple or detailed, they essentially address three key questions:

1 What is our business? Why do we exist?

2 What unique or distinctive competence do we have?

3 What particular franchise or niche will we concentrate on?

THE IMPORTANCE OF "FOCUS": THE CONCEPT OF MARKETING MYOPIA

The medical term myopia (or "blind spot") can provide a useful organisational analogy here.[1] Consider, for example, the story of the railroads in the United States, now a classic in seminars on Strategic Business Planning. Over time the railroads invested huge amounts of capital in refurbishing existing rolling stock and transport communications equipment. Despite this investment, the railways "market-share" declined by 75 per cent over a thirty year period until the 1970s. These declining passenger levels were against a backdrop of ever greater numbers of people travelling. In a time of declining share for the railroads, more and more people were travelling — but by air! The lesson: The railroads had defined their mission in terms of the rail transport industry. If they had widened this boundary and accepted they were in the "travel market", they may have seen the competitive threat from airlines and responded earlier.

A similar story is told about the movie industry in California. Hollywood moguls for a long time defined their mission as "movie making" rather than "entertainment". The evolution of television from the late 1950s marked a "type" change in competition and largely

---

1 The term Marketing Myopia was first coined by Ted Levitt in the *Harvard Business Review* (July-August 1960).

accounts for the fact that much of the television output is now produced on the east coast of the US. David Whitwam, CEO of Whirlpool, makes a similar point in relation to the sale of washing machines: "If you want to open the door to imagination and innovation, isn't it more useful to think of the fabric-care business" (*Harvard Business Review*, 1994).

The above highlights the danger in setting the goalposts too narrowly. However, expansiveness can be equally disastrous through dissipating scarce organisational resources. The key is to find the correct level of focus for the business and this in turn drives all other elements of business strategy.

Many symptoms of corporate failure have their roots in the absence of a clear sense of direction. However, it is not easy to construct a well-boundaried mission statement. Anyone who has ever tried to agree a particular form of wording with a group of people will identify with this. It is vital to avoid the creation of a statement which is banal and obvious. What is certain is that with a well-crafted statement, the organisational benefits far outweigh any difficulties in construction.

 ## ESTABLISHING A "SENSE OF MISSION"

Not all mission statements have a positive impact on performance. Some mission statements exist primarily to decorate annual reports or act as decor in upmarket reception areas (the external public relations function of mission statements) and never permeate the fibre of an organisation. A critical point is that mission statements are probably less important than establishing a "sense of mission" within the management team which is subsequently communicated to the general body of employees. This point is sometimes missed by companies (even those that have experimented with the concept) who often spend too much time on "wordsmithing" and getting a document technically correct. The process of constructing a new mission should be the first step in changing an existing organisation and mobilising the workforce. Well-constructed mission statements are more than simply a definition of business activity; they are a statement of philosophy and purpose.

Organisational mission tends to be stable over time and will only change if there is a major shift in business direction.

 ## MISSION STATEMENT EXAMPLES

Listed below are some actual examples of mission statements. They can range from simple to quite complex statements of purpose.

1 **The Body Shop: Natural Products Retailer** "Sell products which do not hurt animals or the environment".

2 **British Telecom: Telecommunications** "British Telecom's Mission is to provide world class telecommunications and information products and services and to develop and exploit our networks at home and overseas".

3 **TI Group: International Engineering** "TI's strategic thrust is to become an international engineering group concentrating on specialist engineering businesses, operating in selected niches on a global basis. Key businesses must be able to command a position of sustainable technological and market share leadership".

The soul never thinks without a picture

Aristotle

Organisation "vision" can be differentiated from organisation "mission" in one critically important way. While mission details the purpose of the organisation, vision sets a concrete target to be achieved. A soccer analogy may be useful here.

Tranmore Rovers Mission Statement "We want to be a professional Soccer Team".

Tranmore Rovers Vision Statement "We want to play in the Premier League and by end 1997 finish in the top three positions in that League".

The two concepts (mission and vision) have very different purposes. However, not all organisations have two separate statements — they are sometimes combined.[2]

 ORGANISATION VISION: A WORD PICTURE

Organisation vision is a word picture which depicts a possible and desirable future state of an organisation. It is almost a preview of a future Annual Report which is superior to what currently exists. An organisational vision which is well constructed, is a coherent and powerful statement of what the business can and

---

2 There are no single, standard definitions of these terms which are universally applied. This adds to the confusion and debate re their impact on performance and creates some of the scepticism levelled against these terms.

should be in X years time (the actual timeframe will depend on the individual business or industry).

The vision should be short enough to be memorable yet still vividly capture the essence of the organisational purpose. The vision selected by Ford Motor Company in the 1980s was "Quality is Job 1", a simple statement which is difficult to forget or misunderstand (and which may help to explain the turnaround in that company's fortunes in recent times).

Organisation vision statements are often emotionally loaded concepts based on "higher ideals and/or a noble purpose". In some cultures (particularly Japan), vision statements are often based on raw competitive ambition. Some examples:

- **Komatsu**   "Encircle Caterpillar"

- **Canon**   "BX" (Beat Xerox)

- **Fuji**   "Overtake Kodak"

- **Honda**   "Beat Benz"

A critical point about vision is its power to move an organisation in a predetermined direction. The power of a clearly articulated vision statement is that it can allow organisations to reach supposedly "impossible goals". For example, none of the Japanese company visions detailed above now raise an eyelid. However, when they were first outlined (e.g. the Komatsu example) they seemed incredible.

 FOUR SEASONS HOTELS

Four Seasons Hotels provide a textbook example of senior management's unwavering vision. The Toronto chain consistently beats the industry in occupancy rates and repeat business; return on equity has exceeded 20 per cent for the past number of years. Chairman Isadore Sharpe, who started the business in 1960, says: "A single purpose dictates our priorities — to operate the finest hotels in every city in which we're located" (*Fortune*, March 1989).

Another key difference between vision and mission is that the former can change when the goal is reached. Vision statements set relatively short-term targets which inspire the people within an organisation to perform at a higher level until that particular target is reached. As one academic describes it: "It is like running the marathon in 100 yard sprints" (Dr. Maurice Sains, 1992).

▶ VISION WITH A SMALL "V": AN ORGANISATION CHANGE TOOL

Vision, as described above, is a summary statement of an organisational target for some future point. However, the concept of organisational vision can also be understood in another way.[3]

During times of change, organisations usually need to work on a number of issues. Staying with the soccer analogy referred to earlier, in order to get into the top three positions in the Premier League, Tranmore Rovers may need to pursue a number of individual initiatives. For example, they may need to purchase some players to strengthen the team, build a new stand to hold the

---

3 I am indebted to Dr Eddie Molloy for clarifying the role of vision in the context of organisational change.

capacity crowds expected and change their training schedule. A vision statement can be constructed for each of these particular initiatives. This will help the Tranmore Rovers management team to plan the transition projects, moving from "today" to "tomorrow".

Today we are ...	Transition Projects	By 1997 we will be ...
A third division team with a mixture of playing talents	**a** Buy a new goal-keeper **b** Buy a new centre forward	A Premier Division team with excellent soccer skills
Playing in an old ground which cannot cater for our existing level of support and which is both uncomfortable and unsafe	**a** Raise £250,000 in additional funds to improve the ground **b** Visit the best soccer facilities in Europe to see state of the art safety management **c** Commission an architectural competition to redesign the stadium	The most modern soccer ground in the Premier Division, which is completely safe and comfortable and allows scope to significantly develop corporate entertainment
Semi-fit players who often play at less than their potential due to tiredness	**a** Hire the services of a new coach **b** Train every day for four hours, Monday through Friday	The fittest team in the Premier Division

 UNLEASHING THE TALENT OF YOUR PEOPLE

Rosabeth Moss Kanter noted that organisations which shared a common vision between sections were "much quicker to respond to changes in the environment". Those organisations that were strongly segmentalist (i.e. where each part of the organisation was working on its own agenda) were much less able to solve problems as the world around them changed.

The emphasis on a "shared vision" reflects the importance (and difficulty) of translating a boardroom concept to the shop or office floor in a way that inspires positive action. When the vision evolves from the members of the organisation themselves, this potential hurdle gets swept aside and companies who are successful in this area often find some way to "stitch people into" the construction process.

One possibility is to adopt some external criteria as a vision (e.g. achieving the Malcolm Baldbridge Award in the US or acquiring an ISO 9000 seal of approval in Europe). This can be a very useful way to lock people behind a company-wide challenge. Examples of some very graphic visions are outlined on this page.

WHAT ARE ORGANISATIONAL VALUES?

Values are the bedrock of any corporate culture. As the essence of a company's philosophy for achieving success, Values provide a sense of common direction for all employees and guidelines for their day-to-day behaviour

Deal and Kennedy, *Corporate Cultures*

The third element under the Strategic Focus Plan umbrella is the concept of organisational values. Values are a set of individual beliefs or morals which lead to particular behaviours. They are ideals which not alone determine our behaviour but give meaning to our own lives. They are basic assumptions — those things which people in the organisation believe to be absolutely right and true and which affect their behaviour even if they are not always consciously aware of them.

 WHAT, WHERE AND HOW

If the organisation mission provides the "what" (business are we in) and the vision provides the "where" (do we want to get to), then values addresses the "how" (do we wish to behave in getting there). The challenge for management is to build a culture that meshes the desired values (priorities) of individuals with the ideals of the organisation. When this happens, work truly provides meaning and employees are able to willingly commit to the goals of the organisation.

It is important to realise that all organisations have values, whether articulated or not. In some companies, values are openly recognised and sometimes published (see examples below). In other companies, values have to be inferred from management behaviour, company systems, policies and procedures or "artefacts" (everything from office layout to executive toys in managers offices). A listing of "values indicators" is detailed in Appendix A.

► NOBLE VALUES RAISE ENERGY LEVELS

Noble values tend to raise energy levels. People are emotional beings and are energised by goals which stress they are "working for a cause". In earlier times, people worked to pay the mortgage and feed the family. While this is still an issue, rising standards of living have led to a situation whereby many senior employees can "cover the basics" by working on Monday and Tuesday. As managers, how are we to motivate this group for the rest of the week? Articulating values that people can subscribe to can help to deliver "volunteers" to organisations rather than "conscripts".

► THE SHIFT TO FLAT ORGANISATION AND KNOWLEDGE-BASED WORK

Traditionally, commitment to an organisation's goals was achieved through an unquestioning loyalty and obedience to the hierarchical system. Kings and queens, the church, military organisations and, until

Every excellent company we studied is clear on what it stands for, and takes the process of value shaping seriously. In fact, we wonder whether it is possible to be an excellent company without clarity on values and without having the right sort of values

Peters and Waterman, *In Search of Excellence*

recently, modern corporations achieved uniform values through respect for hierarchy. Today, this is no longer possible to the same extent. Members of organisations tend to be more independent and motivated by more democratic principles. They demand the opportunity to grow and reach their potential in the context of the workplace. People want the experience of work to be fulfilling as well as providing a means of paying the bills.

 ## LESSENING THE NEED FOR DIRECT CONTROL

A further organisational benefit is that values lessen the need for supervision through providing indirect control. The concept here is that (as Douglas McGregor highlighted 30 years ago) under the correct conditions people will impose more control upon themselves than can be imposed upon them from outside. Success in the emerging world business order increasingly depends on the capabilities of employees. In many companies, hierarchies are being flattened to tap the potential of individuals. Innovative leaders are creating new structures which encourage collaboration between units without management intervention; the outputs of knowledge-based workers cannot be managed in the same way that blue-collar workers were controlled. These changes place a greater emphasis on the need for leadership which is based on shared values. In this new leadership paradigm, loyalty is given to the shared values, rather than the values of any single person in a position of power.

By meshing the needs of the individual with the needs of the organisation, values-based leadership helps organisations harness greater human resource energy and potential, which in turn allows them to:

• Reduce costs

• Create innovative new products

• Provide a caring service to customers

• Respond quickly to market changes

• Produce any other value which the organisation deems to be necessary in their particular operating environment.

The values of our mythical soccer team, Tranmore Rovers, could be expressed as follows:

• We believe that the safety of our fans is paramount

• We play to win every time

• The team result is more important than individual brilliance.

▶ VALUE STATEMENT EXAMPLES

Examples of some actual values statements are outlined below:

BBA (Scottish industrial engineering company)

1 Budgets are personal commitments made by management to their superiors, subordinates, shareholders and their self-respect

2 The Victorian work ethic is not an antique — go home tired

3 Three years in the current environment is the limit of man's comprehension of what may be.

Sterling Winthrop (Pharmaceutical/Healthcare Company)

1 We are a winning team

2 We are customer driven

3 We are dedicated to continuous improvement

4 We have a sense of urgency

5 We act responsibly.

THE STRATEGIC FOCUS DOCUMENT

Having clearly articulated mission, vision and values statements is, of itself, not enough. You still need a mechanism or a "roadmap", to translate this thinking into concrete day-to-day actions which take you where you want to go to. One mechanism to achieve this is to construct a "Strategic Focus" Document (see Figure 2).

FIGURE 2
Strategic Focus Document

1. Organisation Mission	4. Key Result Areas The areas on which we need to focus our attention.	5. Measurements 1-3 measurements per Key Result Area.		6. Action Plans Individual steps to drive the business towards achieving a "key result".
	A Product Innovation	1. 2. 3.		
2. Organisation Vision	B Marketing Excellence	1. 2. 3.		
	C Productivity through People	1. 2. 3.		
	D Customer Satisfaction	1. 2. 3.		
3. Statement of Values	E World-class Production	1. 2. 3.		
	F Resource Allocation	1. 2. 3.		

▶ WHAT ARE KEY RESULT AREAS?

The notion of "key result areas" is a commercial concept which addresses the question: "What are the Critical Success Factors in this business?" Business is a competitive economic game. Winners have strategies which focus resources on exploiting company strengths and external opportunities. In simple terms, "excellence" is not enough; you need to be excellent in areas of strategic importance.

Key result areas are usually limited in number (four to eight is the norm). These define the distinctive competencies or competitive advantages which a company currently has or wishes to create in the future, and are the areas which need constant management attention. The Index Consulting Group in the US has listed the ten most common categories as follows:

1 Strategic Direction

2 Customer Satisfaction

3 Product Quality and Innovation

4 Production Operations

5 Cost Control and Productivity

6 Management Capability

7 Human Resource Management

8 Culture and Attitude Change

9 Systems and Control

10 External Affairs/Regulatory

McKinsey, another US-based consulting group, has listed an additional three factors:

1 Profitability

2 Market Standing

3 Financial and Physical Resources.

There are few businesses (if any) which would require a key result area which falls outside of the combined listing of 13 factors above. However, the real skill lies in choosing the 4-6 areas which are key to the success of the organisation.

▶ WHAT ARE STRATEGIC MEASUREMENTS?

"Measurements" in the sense used here, are agreed ways to measure progress towards achieving the company mission, vision, values and key result areas. The management idiom "what gets measured gets done" holds true in most cases. Edward Demming reminds us to "expect what you inspect".

Measurements are usually stated in terms of quantity, cost, quality or timeliness.

▶ WHAT IS ACTION PLANNING?

Management offices the world over are filled with Strategic Plans, often beautifully bound, which are long on intellectualism and short on communication and implementation. When updated annually, they have a role in steering the direction of the business but add little value in terms of unleashing the potential of the people within the organisation.

Strategic statements are "empty intellectualism" unless they convert into action. Indeed, in many organisations "strategic thinking" out-distances "strategic capability" because of a failure (and often an inadequacy) to operationalise the strategy. The key to the successful building of a strategic focus is to get people involved in its development and implementation. As one author asked rhetorically: "How would you feel if someone sent you a copy of your New Year's Resolutions?" People do not resist their own ideas. The really smart companies get their people involved in creating tomorrow's strategy and organisation and stand back to count the positive results.

The process of strategically analysing the company and then defining its Mission, Vision and Values lies at the heart of building a high commitment organisation. Management is not as cerebral a process as business schools unwittingly make it out to be with a myriad of frameworks, models and tools. While management certainly demands intellectual and technical skills of the highest level, it is also about managing people — people in search of meaning towards which to direct their efforts.

The concepts of Mission, Vision and Values can provide this meaning. It can help organisations to focus their scarce resources and bind their people around a common identity giving them a sense of destiny. The definition of Mission, Vision and Values has thus moved from being an esoteric human resource technique to the primary leadership challenge for the 1990s and beyond.

Note: A framework to compare *your* organisation to the concepts detailed above is provided in Appendix B.

CHAPTER

2

THE CUSTOMER
IS KING

2.1 INTRODUCTION

There aren't any categories of problems here. There is just one problem. Some of us aren't paying enough attention to our customers

Tom Watson Snr.

When Marie Antoinette's milliner said "there is nothing new except what's been forgotten", she could well have been speaking of customer service. The notion of customer satisfaction is hardly new. People talk about it all the time. The stark reality, though, is that it is one of the most universally underpractised values in business today. In so many companies the customer is "Seen as a nuisance ... whose unpredictable behavior damages carefully made strategic plans, whose activities mess up computer operations, and who stubbornly insists that purchased products should work" (*Business Week*, 1991).

The idea of customers as being a necessary evil ("some businesses see customers as a wallet with a person attached" — Gene Perret) gets communicated in a thousand different ways inside organisations. Translated, it results in poor service with consequent declines in market share and profitability. At the first service company where this author worked, Customer Service Representatives (whose job was to service existing accounts) ranked lowest on the influence totem pole. The thinking: anyone with potential would get a real job (e.g. in accounting or manufacturing)!

IRISH MARKETING GRADUATES

Several Irish marketing students underwent a summer placement in a retail supermarket group. They spent three months getting to know the various elements of the business. At the end of the placement, the *Irish Times* asked the students to assess the benefits of the programme. One remarked: "It was really boring. All we did was meet customers."

In many companies, far from being seen as "king", the vision of customers is less complimentary.

A RENAISSANCE IN CUSTOMER SERVICE

Customer service has undergone somewhat of a renaissance in recent times. The earliest indication of this was the identification of customer service as one of the "Eight Success Factors" in the classic, *In Search Of Excellence* (Peters and Waterman, 1982). Since then there have been a number of titles published on the subject. The message in the literature is surprisingly simple: Excellent service revolves around a bone-deep belief in the importance of customers which is translated each day into thousands of small, customer-focused activities. While all companies give lip service to how much they value their customers, a distinguishing feature of the excellent companies is that they back up their words with intense, positive actions. Every activity is devoted to getting new customers and satisfying existing customers.

The customer-first focus is seen even in areas which are isolated from the market (accounting, engineering, purchasing, personnel, legal, word processing, shipping, reception, even top management). The sheer intensity of customer concern within these companies is unmatched by competitors.

WALKING THE TALK

The excellent service companies stay uncommonly close and committed to their customers. They demonstrate conviction bordering on the irrational that they exist only for the customer. Customer service is not perceived as "the icing on the cake". Excellent customer service companies consider service to be a major competitive advantage, not an "add-on" benefit. Indeed, if you sell a "commodity product" excellent service may be the only way to differentiate yourself from the competition. Lech Walesa told the US congress that there is a declining world market for words. He was right. Excellent customer service is about behaviour, not talk.

CUSTOMER SERVICE ASSUMES EXCELLENT PRODUCT QUALITY

Come give us a taste of your quality

William Shakespeare
Hamlet

Perhaps the denigration of customer service in recent times can be traced to a misunderstanding of the term — the notion that excellence in this area can be achieved by remembering customers' birthdays, children's names and other personal details and exploiting this information at appropriate moments. Nothing could be further from the truth. No company can survive long with a philosophy that could be described as "all wrapping and no present". Excellent customer service is *not* a package of human relations skills or marketing hoopla which provides competitive advantage regardless of the quality of the basic product offering. Excellent customer service *is* conformance to customers' expectations, 100 per cent of the time. If customer satisfaction could be expressed as a ratio, it would look like this.

$$\text{Customer satisfaction} = \frac{\text{Perceived quality of product/service}}{\text{Needs, wants and expectations}}$$

Customers expect washing machines that wash, burgers that taste good and courier services that arrive on time. And more. Most products are wrapped in a "package of services". People don't simply want a washing machine that washes; it should also have a friendly salesperson, be delivered on time and get great back-up if it breaks down after ten years service. Excellent customer service companies recognise the importance of product/service quality in addition to the package of ancillary services which accompany this. It's not just what you get but how you get it that is measured by the customer.

 PREMIER INDUSTRIAL CORPORATION

Early one afternoon in late 1988, Premier Industrial Corporation got a call from the manager of a Caterpillar tractor plant in Decatur, Illinois. A $10 electrical relay had broken down, idling an entire assembly line. A sales representative for Premier, a distributor of industrial parts, located a replacement at the company's Los Angeles warehouse and rushed it to a plane headed for St. Louis. By 10.30 that night, a Premier employee had delivered the part and the line was up and running. "You can't build tractors if you can't move the line", says Vern Jordan, a Caterpillar purchasing analyst. "They really saved us a whole lot of money."

Such service levels are very expensive, but it pays off. Premier can charge up to 50 per cent more than competitors for every one of the 250,000 mundane industrial parts it stocks, and its return on equity was a healthy 27.8 per cent on sales of $596 million in 1989. Says co-founder and Chairman, Morton L. Mandel: "To us, customer service is the main event".

SOUNDS GREAT BUT DOES IT INFLUENCE RESULTS?

Looking after your customers is not merely good manners — it's good business too

Scottish Proverb

There is substantial evidence to answer a resounding "yes" to the above. Specific example: The Japanese were the first to recognise the problem of declining customer service. In the 1970s, they started to rescue customers from their limbo of so-so merchandise and "take it or leave it" service. They built loyalty in the US by assiduously uncovering and accommodating customer needs.

In 1973, Toyota Motor Corporation opened a design centre in Southern California to fine-tune its cars for American tastes. The results from this and other similar initiatives was a direct, positive impact on their bottom line. Studies by Forum Corporation, a Boston-based consulting firm that specialises in consumer service, show that keeping an existing customer typically costs only one-fifth as much as acquiring a new one. It is not surprising, therefore, that companies known for customer satisfaction often outperform their competitors.

GOOD MONEY FROM GOOD SERVICE

The table below contrasts "industry bests" vs "industry averages".

	Avg. Annual sales growth 1987–89 %	Avg. return on equity * 1987–89 ** %
American Express	14.4	18.3
All Financial Services	13.3	15.6
AMR	20.3	12.0
All Airlines	14.6	– 0.5
Ford Motor Company	15.3	23.3
All Auto Manufacturing	9.2	13.1
3M	11.7	19.8
All General Manufacturing	14.0	14.7

* Common stockholders only

Source: Data Compustat Inc.   ** 1989 data estimated

Despite the overriding evidence that a customer service orientation strategy is critical for commercial success, it is not easy to engender this thinking in an established organisation. As one wry commentator noted: "Birth, after all, is infinitely easier than resurrection" (Aburdene and Naisbitt, 1985).

Yet despite the difficulties, companies searching for ways to make their organisations more customer-driven can take some simple lessons from the world's best. The 5-Step Model outlined below captures the core philosophy and working practices of excellent customer-service companies around the globe.

FIGURE 1
The Customer is King

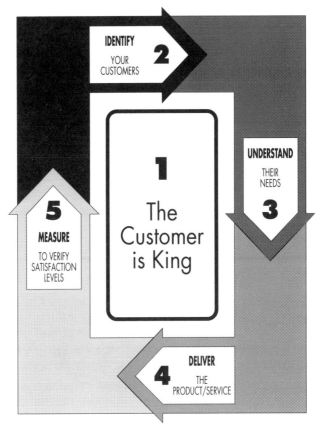

STEP 1:
ESTABLISH A CUSTOMER SERVICE VISION

Serve and Sell

Early IBM slogan

The first step in excellent customer service lies in creating a clear vision of how your company will operate.

 MOTOROLA

When Chairman Robert Galvin visited customers in late 1986, he heard complaints that Motorola was hard to do business with. Galvin realised he had work to do, so he agreed that "Total Customer Satisfaction" should be the topic of Motorola's 1988 Senior Executive Program (a series of presentations and workshops held annually with 200 senior executives to discuss important issues affecting the company). What emerged from the meetings, says senior vice president Kenneth Hessler, "was the realisation that we had lost something. We were being driven by cost saving instead of taking care of the customer." The reaction was swift. All executives received pagers so that their large corporate customers could reach them day or night. Motorola recently authorised its field service crew to repair all their customers' defective pagers, two-way radios, and mobile phones on the spot without home office approval if the work costs $1,000 or less. The communications sector has also revamped its compensation, so that buyers' satisfaction figures in every manager's bonus as well as the salesperson's. Motorola's phone and mail surveys indicate that customer satisfaction has risen significantly in the past two years.

SCANDINAVIAN AIRLINES (SAS)

In 1980, Jan Carlzon, as president of SAS made headlines world-wide. He managed to turn around the company from an operating loss of $20 million to a gross profit of more than $70 million. Key to this success was the establishment of a customer service vision captured in the now famous "moments of truth" concept.

Carlzon saw every encounter with a customer as a moment of truth with two possible outcomes — either positive or negative. His vision was a positive outcome for every SAS customer and this became the target for all employees. In 1986, he estimated that each of the company's 10 million customers came into contact with approximately five SAS employees, with each contact lasting an average of 15 seconds. Thus: "SAS is created 50 million times a year, 15 seconds at a time. Those 50 million moments of truth are the moments that ultimately determine whether SAS will succeed or fail as a company. They are the moments when we must prove to our customers that SAS is their best alternative."

SEEING CUSTOMERS AS APPRECIATING ASSETS

In *Thriving On Chaos* Tom Peters suggests that companies should consider customers as appreciating assets:

"When the Federal Express courier enters my office, she should see $180,000 stamped on the forehead of our receptionist. My little twenty-five-person firm runs about a $1,500-a-month Fed Ex bill. Over ten years, that will add up to $180,000. I suggest that this simple device, calculating the ten-year (or, alternatively, lifetime) value of a customer can be very powerful and has sweeping implications."

There is no standard formula for setting customer service (or any other) company vision. The ideal very much depends on the particular environment, the stamp which the top team wishes to put on a company and the current state of the business. What is certain, however, is that without a defined customer service vision, it is increasingly difficult to ensure that the people who currently buy your products or services will continue to do so in the longer term. Setting a clear "customer is king" vision is the first step in ensuring long-term positive customer relations.

For small, single product companies customer identification seems like a "no brainer" exercise. It's not. For larger companies and those that have a more diverse product or service portfolio, it is an even more difficult exercise. One exercise used in customer service workshops is to ask managers to list their customers. Very often they have difficulty or experience confusion with what seems like a simple request. The choices made usually range across the person's direct boss, peer group, an internal department to which service is given and the "external" customer. Who then is the "real" customer?

▶ INTERNAL CUSTOMER SERVICE: THE FORGOTTEN HEROES

Knowing your customer is relatively simple if you are a waiter in Raffles Hotel or a Key Account Manager for Amex in Cairo. However, not all work is as clearly customer service-focused. If you are a research chemist, operating with a group of scientists on the toxicology of a chemical which is ten years away from becoming a pharmaceutical product, "who is my customer" becomes a much more difficult question. For many employees, particularly those in large, non-front-line-service-sections, the "external customer" can seem a very distant being.

"To make a pair of shoes requires more than a hundred pair of hands, and many products are far more complex than this. It is hardly surprising, therefore, that sometimes people within the process feel that they are distant from and have no clear perception of, the end user" (Robinson, 1986).

In bigger companies only a small percentage of employees may have direct contact with the external customer. If people are unsure of who their customer is, how can such companies instill a philosophy of "the customer is king"? The lesson here revolves around a company's ability to promote the internal customer as being just as important as external service. Internal service departments provide services earlier in the "value-added" chain. Like any chain, each link needs to be fully competent. While the ultimate customer is always external, services along the internal chain must be excellent to ensure the final output can match world-class standards.

STERLING DRUG

Sterling Drug provided a good example of how to overcome the "customer anonymity" that many large companies face. Firstly, customer service was defined as a core company value and strenuous efforts were made to communicate this throughout the organisation. Secondly, in Sterling's definition of customer service, equal weight was given to servicing of "internal" customers on the basis that over 80 per cent of Sterling's people had an internal person as their primary customer. The key message was that each "internal" transaction had to be completed effectively in order that the final "external" customer transaction provided added value.

▶ VISITS WITH CUSTOMERS

In order to engender a marketplace focus, Caterpillar sends people from its manufacturing plants out to watch "the big machines at play". Citibank encourages "back room" operations people to regularly visit customers. 3M and Hewlett Packard insist that their R&D people regularly meet customers, often as sales representatives in retail outlets that sell their products. A wonderful example of this was designed in Sterling's operation in the Philippines where plant employees were encouraged to adopt their local neighbourhood drugstore. Each employee became responsible for conducting service audits within their local community (a standard checklist helped employees to conduct the audits). Not surprisingly, customer service levels as measured across a range of indices improved dramatically. Through these simple contacts with external customers, the service orientation becomes tangible and the phrase "each of us is the company" takes on a real meaning.

Let deeds

correspond with

words

Plautus

Excellent customer service companies have a range of devices to ensure they tap into their customers' requirements. They build redundancy into their listening systems to ensure nothing of importance gets through the net. As Karl Albrecht and Ron Zemke described it: "These organisations seem to wear both belts and suspenders, just in case" (1985).

In addition to the usual bank of formal market research tools, excellent customer service companies utilise a plethora of "informal" mechanisms, some of which are listed below.

 ## MBWA WITH CUSTOMERS

The term MBWA (Management By Wandering Around) is a publicised aspect of the employee relations philosophy at Hewlett Packard, but lends itself equally well to the customer service arena. Where the customer is truly "king", people go out and meet with customers, listen to their needs and assess their aspirations. It is done regularly and everyone gets involved (not just marketing personnel). MBWA avoids the "Taj Mahal" syndrome whereby companies become distant from their reason for being — customer service.

We never really

ask. We don't.

We survey. We

panel. We visit.

We parade. But

we don't

L-I-S-T-E-N. Not

with a novice ear

Tom Peters

In the excellent customer service companies, subjective feedback is given at least equal billing to statistical analysis and active listening is practised, not the selling of pet ideas.

▶ SONY

When Sony researched the market for a lightweight, portable cassette player, results showed that customers would not buy a tape recorder that did not record. Company chairman, Akio Morita, decided to introduce the Walkman anyway and the rest is history. Today it is one of Sony's most successful products.

The "soft data" approach to market research may seem to lack the methodological rigor of scientific methods, but it is by no means haphazard or careless. Measures such as customer reaction and dealer enthusiasm can only be observed first hand. These are critical factors in the successful marketing of some products and often missed in statistical analysis. There is a secondary benefit here: companies who actually visit customers as part of their market research, can build lasting relationships with their customers all along the distribution chain. Why? Because so many companies are tied up dealing with internal processes. They become deskbound and lose sight of their basic *raison d'être*, — customer service

▶ DuPONT

By listening to everyone who helps get goods to the market, DuPont turned Stain Master stain resistant carpeting into the most successful new-product introduction in its history, bigger even than nylon. To develop the Stain Master fibre (which is sold to mills that weave it into carpet), Tom McAndrews, director of DuPont's flooring systems division, appointed a six member committee of marketing. R&D and financial people. He told them to ask themselves constantly: "How does what we're doing affect the customer?"

Before Stain Master was introduced, the committee spent three years coordinating closely with retailers and mill operators by regularly asking them for suggestions about how to price Stain Master and publicise its benefits to the consumer. As a result, Du Pont launched the product with the company's largest advertising campaign ever for a new product. The fibre has revived carpet sales industry-wide and produced over $2 billion in revenues.

"The key is we looked at our customers as the entire distribution chain. You can't simply meet the needs of the end user."

► FORD

Ford surveys some 2.5 million customers a year and regularly invites owners to meet engineers and dealers to discuss quality problems. It has also designed a software system that makes it easier for executives and engineers to use customer-satisfaction data. Ford chairman, Donald E. Peterson, said: "If we aren't customer driven, our cars won't be either." On target, but Ford's customer follow-through still doesn't match Nissan's. Every customer who buys or services a vehicle at a Nissan Motor Corp. dealership gets a call from an outside research firm to see how they were treated.

Ford's decade-long effort shows how tough it is to transform a company into an operation obsessed with pleasing customers at every stage. Hyatt President Thomas J. Pritzker says there's a fallacy that customer service can just be turned on. "Management has to set a tone and then constantly push, push."

LISTEN TO LEAD USERS

Tom Peters advises that you should seek out and listen to those customers demanding the most up-to-date products and services and those most likely to already be trying things with top flight competitors. Question them about potential ideas and improvements. Test ideas on them and have them evaluate (and participate in) your experiments. Bring them into the company's "family". Find out what their skunkworks are up to. What problems are they trying to solve because you and your competitors have not yet solved them?

Michael Porter, the Harvard Business School professor, expresses it as follows:

OLD MICHAEL PORTER WISDOM
Seek out easy customers who are not price sensitive and who have little choice in who they buy from.

NEW MICHAEL PORTER WISDOM
Seek out the most demanding customers who have most choice.

LINK THE LISTENING DEVICES AND THE ACTION FOLLOW-UP

Most companies contain treasures of customer ideas collected by sales and field service people. What they lack are devices for ensuring that this information makes its way into the design/experimentation/production loop and is not written off as just "wishful thinking by the sales force". Better still, get some customer feedback first hand by doing a front-line job.

▶ DOING FRONT LINE JOBS

Sometimes what you do is ringing so loudly in my ears, I cannot hear what you say

John Powell S.J.

To learn more about customer service, executives in many companies are putting in stints at the front line. At Xerox Corporation, executives spend one day a month taking complaints from customers about machines, bills and service. At Hyatt hotels, senior executives — including President Pritzker — put in time as bellhops. In Superquinn, the premier Irish retail supermarket group, Feargal Quinn the Managing Director spends time packing bags for the customers. He calls it "jumping the counter", seeing the store from the customer's perspective.

Such practices give access to the reality of customer satisfaction in a way that statistical measures can never communicate. They also have a tremendous secondary benefit — they role model customer service principles to employees much more effectively than team briefings or internal newsletters can.

STEP 4:
DELIVER THE PRODUCT OR SERVICE

*Nothing
succeeds like
excess*

Oscar Wilde

Creating real and perceived excellent service means, above all, doing a thousand little things well. Attention to a myriad of small details determines the difference between satisfied and irritated customers. This translates into delivering what is promised and more, even if it requires "over-extending" to do so. It takes continuous extra effort and doesn't always result in an immediate incremental sale.

Excellent companies rely on the commitment of all their people to provide uncompromised service. From the receptionist to the marketing representative, from the accounting department to the shopfloor, everyone is considered accountable to provide complete customer satisfaction. It is an ingrained belief.

▶ TECHNOLOGY AS A COMPETITIVE WEAPON

Several companies use technology as a competitive weapon in the excellent customer service revolution. The SAS goal of meeting take-off deadlines was partly accomplished through the "Moment of Truth" vision and partly by the purchase of de-icing equipment. Hotel computers which allow operators to answer with the guest's name each time an internal call is made is a particularly good example of this. However, technology can also be misapplied, resulting in an increasingly impersonal environment with customers thwarted by well intentioned but misguided applications. The earlier points made regarding treating customers as individuals holds good here.

 ## CUSTOMERS ARE HUMAN

The general attitude about service is an interesting paradox. While everybody wants it, most don't want to give it

Buck Rodgers – IBM

A favourite customer service story concerns the purchase of five pieces of optical equipment, each costing just under $25,000. About a week after they had arrived, the customer found that they could not be used as the electrical contact points (a small part costing less than $5) were damaged. He phoned the supplier and was told that the equipment had left the factory in full working order. In a series of letters which followed, the supplier went on to "prove" that the parts were damaged by the customer's personnel. Eventually, the customer relented and agreed that the damage was indeed caused by his people. He then cancelled the order. When asked to explain, he said that commercially it was an unsound decision "but I just won't buy anything from that son of a bitch". In customer service terms, being wrong may sometimes be right.

 ## UNDER-PROMISE AND OVERDELIVER

Most of us want to create a good impression with our customers. Because of this we tend to overpromise. Leading Edge Products Inc. learned this particular lesson the hard way. The maker of IBM PC clones which was eventually plucked out of Chapter 11 by Daewoo Telcom Co., it was the one to beat several years ago. Besides low price, the company offered a 15-month guarantee — 12 months more than the competition. But after diversification drained cash, and management attention, it simply could not fill orders. And when its machines acted up consumers couldn't get help. Leading Edge "was a victim of their own marketing success," says Robert Orbachm, Director of Business Development of 47th Street Photo in New York. "They couldn't live up to the expectation they set." Contrast this with the IBM vignette below.

▶ IBM

A service rep based in Phoenix was driving to Tempe to deliver a small part a customer needed to restore a malfunctioning data centre. But what was usually a short, pleasant drive turned into a nightmare. Torrential rains transformed the Salt River into rampaging rapids, which closed all but two of the sixteen bridges that crossed over to Tempe, causing a bumper to bumper traffic jam that changed the normal 25 minute drive to a four hour crawl. Determined not to lose the entire afternoon to the traffic, the service rep remembered that she had a pair of roller skates in the trunk of her car. She pulled out of the line of traffic, donned the skates, and skated across the bridge and to the customer's rescue (Rodgers, 1986).

A successful policy of customer focus has to start with a strong commitment from top executives. But for all the inspirational work by CEOs, the nitty-gritty of satisfying customers often falls to sales clerks and factory workers.

▶ MARRIOTT CORPORATION

Marriott knows that workers who deal directly with customers can make or break a marketing programme. For years, Marriott's room-service business didn't live up to its potential. But after initiating a 15-minute delivery guarantee for breakfast in 1985, Marriott's breakfast business — the biggest portion of its room-service revenue — jumped 25 per cent. Marriott got employees to devise better ways to deliver the meals on time, including having deliverers carry walkie-talkies so they could receive instructions more quickly. This specific example mirrors a general trend in high performance companies — empowerment — putting control and responsibility for customer service down the line.

FOUR SEASONS HOTELS

A man without a smiling face should not open a shop

Chinese Proverb

The customer may not always be right, but employees are encouraged to err on his or her side. Says executive vice president John Sharpe: "No one will ever criticise a staffer for making a guest happy."

Four Seasons managers like to tell employees the story of Roy Dyment, a doorman in Toronto who neglected to load a departing guest's briefcase in his taxi. The doorman called the guest, a lawyer in Washington, DC, and discovered that he desperately needed the briefcase for a morning meeting. Dyment hopped on a plane and returned it — without first securing approval from his boss. The company named Dyment "Employee of the Year".

PROVIDING EXCELLENT SERVICE TO ALL CUSTOMERS

Excellent service companies treat customers as individuals. We all like it when we are treated individually, in a restaurant, a department store or when getting your car serviced. At IBM they call this concept "Being Big — Acting Small".

Too many companies apply the Pareto principle to customer service — good service gets based on the 80/20 rule. While this may have a strong outward rationale to managers with limited resources, it sends a mixed signal to employees. Customer service has to become a core organisational belief, regardless of the order size.

STEP 5:
VERIFY THE LEVEL OF SATISFACTION

We thought the problem was strategic mispositioning! In reality it was that nobody answered the damned phones!

"The final step in our customer service model is to verify the level of satisfaction. Once the product or service is delivered, the need to understand your customers' perception becomes critical. Waiting for complaints is a poor mechanism as the average business never hears from 96 per cent of its customers" (Band, 1991).

Excellent service companies use customers' complaints both as an opportunity to learn about their own organisation and to strengthen loyalty.

 PRITCHARD

"When a client in the City complained one Friday recently," recalls Pritchard manager David Openshaw, "no less than eight senior managers, including the Managing Director, turned up over the weekend, to make sure it was put right before Monday morning" (Clutterbuck and Goldsmith, 1985).

 DOMINOS PIZZA

Privately-held Domino's, which is the world's largest pizza delivery chain, has an effective way to measure satisfaction. It pays 10,000 "mystery customers" $60 each to buy 12 pizzas throughout the year at its 5,000 units and evaluate quality and service. Domino's managers' compensation is partly based on the scores achieved. The central lesson: prune bureaucracy so that customers can talk to you.

GENERAL ELECTRIC

Many consumer experts consider the GE Answer Centre the best 800-number network. Since the company first installed its 800 number, calls have escalated from 1,000 to 65,000 a week. The company value the centre so highly (as a method of getting direct customer feedback) that it has raised the requirements for the 150 phone representatives. They now have to hold a college degree and have sales experience. GE puts each telephone representative through an intensive six-week training program. The centre costs GE more than $10 million a year to operate, but the company figures that payback from the incremental sales is more than twice that amount.

WHAT GETS MEASURED GETS DONE!

Count what is countable, measure what is measurable and what is not measurable make measurable

Galileo

The simple axiom, "what gets measured, gets done," has striking validity. Excellent customer service companies set service goals and establish service measures. Service as an objective can be highly motivating for employees. By singling out and focusing on service measures (from the host of other potential measures), employees will focus on improving service. Yet a caveat has to be inserted here. Don't overfocus on hard data (on time shipments, inventory levels, retail sales etc.). Keep talking to your customers to denote their "perception" of service levels.

▶ FRITO-LAY

Frito-Lay offers its customers a 99.5 per cent service level. All stores (from a tiny Mom and Pop in Oregon to a flagship Safeways in California) stand the same chance of getting a daily call (99.5 per cent) from its Frito routeperson.

▶ RECOGNITION PROVIDES REINFORCEMENT WHICH ENSURES CONTINUITY

The above is psychology 101. Everyone knows it. Yet few companies manage to build it into their remuneration systems and continually reward A while hoping for B. In companies where the customer is "king", top service performers from all functions are recognised on a regular basis, especially for the "little things". The letters, prizes, plaques and badges all serve to recognise superior service performance and market this internally within the organisation. Moreover, such recognition is given to accountants and people in manufacturing almost as regularly as to field service personnel. Unfortunately, too few companies recognise and reward individual performance being chained to a historical fear of upsetting relativities. The lesson is simple: Reinforce good behavior and it will continue; don't and it will be extinguished. Recognition and reinforcement provide the final link in the "customer is king" cycle of organisational excellence.

CONCLUSION

Sadly, we are not moving towards a service economy, but a no-service economy

Thomas R. Horton
A.M.A.

Almost everyone now agrees that paying attention to customers is a critical element of organisational success. But as Robert Waterman notes: "Cultivating the customer is a lot harder than most managers think." For getting close to the customer, he gives the typical US company a 5 on a scale of 1 to 10 — up from a 2 in 1982. Concludes Chairman Stanley Gault: "There's no magic formula for staying close to your customer. It's basic consideration, time, effort, commitment, and follow-up."

It seems so simple. Businesses exist to serve customers and should bend over backward to satisfy their needs. But too many companies still don't get it. In the 1990s more customers are likely to take the opportunity to reward the ones that do.

A checklist against which you can measure the Customer Service provided by your organisation is detailed in Appendix C.

ORGANISATIONAL STRUCTURE

OVERVIEW

In any listing of "factors for organisational success" organisational structure seldom features prominently.[1] In our experience the importance of structure in driving organisation performance is very much underrated. Yet the development of a high performance organisation presupposes good organisational design. Structure has a huge impact on the successful functioning of all organisations; it acts as an "invisible hand", steering underlying business processes and many of the outward behaviours exhibited.

This section attempts to highlight the importance of organisational structure in developing high performance organisations. In order to substantiate this, we detail several underlying principles of organisational design with specific examples of how these work in practise.

These principles provide a relatively simple "Structural Roadmap" that any competent management team can use as a guideline. It will allow you to evaluate an existing structure and provide an "option's menu" to consider when articulating a new structure. Before we move on to explore our "Top 20" principles of effective organisation design, it is useful to define the term "organisational structure" in some more detail.

---

1 Note: This entire chapter was co-written with Dr Eddie Molloy.

ORGANISATIONAL STRUCTURE: WHAT IS IT?

We believe that organisational structure can best be conceptualised as three interrelated components:

1 **The Boxes** This details the formal organisation chart, the principal divisions of work and the reporting relationships. To use a computer analogy, this is the hardware of organisational structure.

2 **Business Processes and Rhythms** The means by which work is organised and the various components of the organisation interact. It is the pattern of meetings, goal setting (both long and short-term) and review mechanisms, the extent of teamwork etc. Staying with the computer analogy this is the software of organisational structure. This particular element of structure often receives scant attention but is a critically important element of organisational effectiveness.

3 **People** The individual "players" who inhabit the boxes (in computer terms, the operators).

Effective organisations, like good computer systems, need all three components to be in harmony.

PROWESS IN STRUCTURING AS A COMPETITIVE WEAPON

Given the rate of change in the business environment, prowess in designing effective organisation structures can become a competitive weapon. In 1983 the Royal Dutch Shell company conducted a survey of the Fortune 500 companies, contrasting this with the listing of companies that were in existence in 1970. The result: During this 13 year period an incredible 33 per cent of these huge companies had disappeared (through mergers, buy-outs and close downs). The average organisational life cycle was 40 years, about half the normal life span of a person. Peter Drucker, in several recent writings, has made a similar point highlighting shortening organisational life cycles as a key trend; in organisations, change is the only certainty and is coming in ever more frequent waves. Across several industries, product life cycles are dramatically shortening and the organisations that support these are in constant turmoil. The rate of change at the macro level is evidenced by changing departmental relationships and grading structures. Overall there is a movement from structures based on functions (Finance, Production, Quality, etc.) to product, market, process and channel-based organisation design.

One noted organisation change expert likens it to managing in "white water", an analogy that will be familiar to anyone who had ever attempted canoeing. The ultimate competitive weapon is therefore not a particular product-market position, but the organisational capacity to respond to these changes (Rosabeth Moss-Kanter, 1993). Skill in organisational re-structuring can, therefore, of itself become a competitive weapon in a turbulent marketplace.

This "capacity to respond" is essentially an organisational ability to re-group, to restructure, to "address the new game". In most cases technological or financial weakness does not explain why many of the company "greats" have fallen on hard times recently (including several of the companies that had been rated as "excellent" during the 1980s); in our experience organisation, or rather the inability to re-organise, is often the Achilles Heel.

A key learning point for Western business is that the great strength of the Japanese is their organisational prowess. While they have seldom been the inventors of new technologies, they are major innovators in structural configurations (Quality Circles, JIT management, TQM, Zig-Zag Career Structures, Heavyweight Product Managers, Lean Production and numerous other structural breakthroughs). The Japanese have developed a skill in structuring and have used this as a key competitive weapon.

Reducing all of the above to its simplest form, companies can outperform the competition through superior structuring. A high level of skill in organisation design should therefore rate in equal importance to capital appraisal, strategic marketing, operational effectiveness and the other core managerial skills. It also follows that a management team should acquire the necessary "organisation design" expertise to outperform the competition by using this key performance lever. Is there then "one best way" to design high performance organisations?

 ## IS THERE "ONE BEST WAY"?

Those who seek simplistic solutions when designing high performance organisations will be disappointed. There is no "one best way" to design an organisation in the same way that there is no "one best way" to design a house. Organisation design is most often a trade-off of principles (e.g. the speed of small independent units versus the scale economies of large enterprises). However, architects design buildings based on specific construction and engineering principles; as a manager a set of underlying design principles is also available to help you design your organisation.

The specific design chosen will be influenced by the nature of the particular task and the uncertainty of the external environment. Abattoirs need a different organisation structure than pharmaceutical research & development laboratories. Both in turn need to be structurally diverse from a multi-store supermarket operation. However, they all share the common features of division of labour into various tasks to be performed and the co-ordination of these tasks to accomplish the activity. Under each heading, organisations have design options.

Listed below are 20 key principles of effective organisational design and the supporting rationale underlying each point. While there are many more principles that could be elaborated, this listing provides the key areas of focus.

The most fundamental principle of organisation design is that "form follows function". This means that structure (form) is dictated by the work or tasks that need to be carried out to provide a logical division of the workload.

This principle means that structure should not be based on history ("that's the way we always did it"), capabilities ("we don't have anyone capable of doing that job") or personalities/personal preferences ("where will we put George?").

▶ SPECIFIC EXAMPLE

In one large pharmaceutical company, a new President was appointed to head up the North American operation ($800 million annual sales). After a short time in the new role the manager announced an organisational structure change. Henceforth a weekly meeting on strategic marketing was to be held — supposedly a key success element to turnaround the business. Because of his successful background in strategic planning and his personal preference for staying in close contact with the planning process, all operations managers were mandated to attend this long (up to 3 hours) meeting at the start of each work week. After some months of very unfruitful meetings, the manager was persuaded to discontinue this weekly forum, to delegate planning to the planners and to hold a twice year-ly strategic review in which all managers participated. Reluctantly he agreed.

The lesson: Personal preferences are not a sound basis for organisational structure decisions.

▶ KEY STRUCTURAL QUESTIONS

• Does the current structure provide a logical division of work?

• If this were a greenfield site what structural configuration would the organisation have?

• How does the current configuration compare with the industry standard?

• Does the current structure reflect the "best fit" with the external environment (by channel, market, product etc.)?

KEY PRINCIPLE 2: REFLECT/CLARIFY ACCOUNTABILITY FOR CRITICAL SUCCESS FACTORS

Critical success factors are those areas that an organisation needs to manage especially well. Organisations need to be excellent in areas of strategic importance. Each of the critical success factors in an organisation should be clearly reflected in the organisation structure and have an identifiable owner.

▶ SPECIFIC EXAMPLES

Bank of Ireland Credit Card Services is strongly committed to excellence in customer service. This company value is reflected in the organisational structure in a number of ways. Firstly, there is a Customer Service Manager with specific responsibility for this area. Secondly, the annual objectives for each manager include customer service measures. Finally, an established tracking process is in place to allow the organisation to check "how are we doing" in relation to a range of integrated customer service metrics that run across all functions. These interrelated and mutually supportive mechanisms give tangible substance to the goal of being "customer driven".

In contrast, a large multi-national subsidiary in the South-West had also named "customer service" as a key company goal. However, the "espoused value" of customer service did not match the on-the-ground reality. In this organisation, the manager in charge of customer services was seen as the weakest member of the management team. The physical space given to the customer service group was poor *vis-à-vis* other sections. In addition, the rates of pay for people working in the customer service area were low *vis-à-vis* comparable jobs in the company (the jobs had been given a lower "points rating"). It is not a major surprise that when an external customer service audit was conducted, the company was deemed "poor" under almost all of the headings surveyed.

KEY STRUCTURAL QUESTIONS

- Are all the strategically important issues represented in the structure?

- Are there newly emerging critical success factors which are not adequately reflected in the structure, e.g. innovation, IT, quality?

- Is there clear ownership of each important performance measure/goal?

- Are there particularly unique features in the company's environment which need to be reflected in the structure?

- How is performance against the Critical Success Factors tracked?

KEY PRINCIPLE 3:
FORESHADOW THE FUTURE

Organisational structure should foreshadow and accelerate progress towards the future. In our experience most organisations are working with a structure that has outlived its "shelf life". There is a story told of a visitor to the West Point Military Academy who, as he entered and later left the Officers Mess for lunch, noticed a soldier standing outside the door. When he enquired of his hosts what the soldier was doing there, he was told "he's there to hold the horses". In similar vein, many business organisational structures have long ceased to be relevant.

As product life cycles shorten, the redesign of individual elements within organisations needs to take place at an ever increasing pace; the ultimate competitive weapon may be responsiveness through structural flexibility. Yet many people in organisations bemoan structural changes as if the disruption caused is not "worth the pain" or that, de facto, previous structural changes did not get it "right". Overall there is an unrealistic expectation that structural changes should be relatively permanent and that too frequent changes are inherently wrong.

Part of the explanation here may be the general aversion to change ("the only person who really agrees with change is a baby with a wet nappy") but it is also rooted in a misunderstanding of the nature of organisational structure and the related timing ("shelf life") of this. It follows that structure should not simply be current but should reflect corporate intentions and trends, e.g. to grow a new business or to move in some new direction. Translating a "vision of tomorrow" into reality requires structural support today. The future is rarely given sufficient attention in organisation design. By the use of embryonic structures — in the form of task forces, an "office" of "X", a project manager, etc., structure becomes an instrument for progressing towards management's vision. If the local management of a manufacturing plant in Sligo establish an opportunity to become a centre for financial management services to all European sites by the end of 1997, now is the time to develop the embryonic structure for that function.

SPECIFIC EXAMPLE

An Irish educational establishment has believed for over two years that its future growth will come from overseas, with up to 30 per cent of its students being from other countries by the year 2000. To date no progress has been made in developing this aspect of the business. The clear reason is that there is no formal structural accountability for this agenda. An embryonic structure established now would accelerate progress towards that vision. You cannot burden existing (often already stretched) resources with a new agenda in an informal manner.

KEY STRUCTURAL QUESTIONS

• How long is the current structure in place?

• Are the goals outlined in the organisation's strategic plans reflected in the current organisation structure?

- Is there an inability to handle new matters/change because of current organisational problems?

- If progress on an agenda already defined some time ago is slow, could it be because you have not structured for it?

KEY PRINCIPLE 4:
THE CREATION OF "SLACK"

Closely related to the notion that structure should foreshadow the future is the creation of sufficient organisational "slack". The concept of "slack" was introduced by Jay Galbraith, an American authority on organisation design. It means that an organisation may choose to be less efficient for a period — by shooting for less ambitious targets or by having additional people around — but, for a purpose. For example, an organisation may carry additional finished product (and bear the increased cost of this) in order to provide 24-hour replenishment for customers. In this case the slack inventory serves a higher order organisation purpose — customer service.

In the context of our discussion on organisation structure that foreshadows the future, the creation of "slack" is essential to:

- do the strategic thinking

- put good people behind key initiatives and opportunities

- innovate, experiment

- create the embryonic structures which will underpin future profitable or otherwise beneficial activity

- create the management and technical strength/depth which organisations need to run a more diverse portfolio — and one that will continually evolve.

Multi-national subsidiaries, especially those which are involved in manufacturing, are typically subject to tight headcount, overhead, travel and many other constraints. Typically they cannot create the "slack" necessary to address their "strategic agenda". It is no coincidence that the third most efficient plant in Digital world-wide, i.e. Clonmel, was closed down a couple of years ago; there is no future in being the most efficient "Pony Express" company, so to speak, while the telephone is being developed back at the ranch. In relative terms, where labour costs are currently £1 an hour in Mullingar, they are 30p in Taiwan and 10p in Shanghai. Those multi-national subsidiaries that are not currently developing their "strategic thinking" are therefore heavily exposed to threats to their continued survival, most often from sister sites within the same organisation. While the concept of strategic thinking for subsidiaries of multi-nationals is outside the scope of this book, it does impact on this specific factor. Without the necessary "slack" it is always difficult to remember that you also have to "drain the swamp" (at least in the longer term), while continuing to shoot the immediate crocodiles.

Again to emphasise, "slack" is spare capacity for a purpose — so it isn't really spare. Where managing future opportunities is a necessary part of the survival game, a company has to become adept at the generation and deployment of managerial resources. It is not usually considered legitimate for a subsidiary to start pursing these wider goals if their performance of the operational charter is below par. The basics must be excellent before a subsidiary can start to address its broader strategic contribution.

▶ SPECIFIC EXAMPLE

Pepsi run a concentrate manufacturing plant in Little Island, just outside Cork city. In addition to creating a world-class manufacturing environment in Cork, the management team have identified a number of "strategic opportunities" outside Ireland (supporting the bottlers distribution channel, working on the construction of new Pepsi sites, etc.). In order to meet the increasing demand for managerial and technical resources, the company recently decided to recruit a number of graduate engineers as "seed labour" to capitalise on future strategic opportunities. These graduates are "slack" in the sense that there is no current "on-site" identified role for them to perform.

▶ KEY STRUCTURAL QUESTIONS

- Do your senior staff have enough time to think about "draining the swamp"?

- Are there opportunities arising which you simply cannot address because all of your good people are overstretched?

- Has the organisation dedicated resources to pursue its strategic agenda? If you were given a gift of five bright, qualified people, what could they do for you?

KEY PRINCIPLE 5:
CLIENT-FACING STRUCTURE

The most obvious omission in most organisational charts is the *raison d'être* — the customer. Organisational structures are normally designed to facilitate the internal flow of work and are not consciously designed to meet the needs of an external audience. Companies therefore need to consider their structure from an "outside-in" perspective which reflects their particular market, evolving customer needs and the channels of distribution. One senior training practitioner (banking sector) recently described his own organisation as follows: "For far too long our managers have had their face to the boss and their a .... to the customer".

Designing organisations from the "outside in" has a number of specific implications which go way beyond the conducting of focus groups or the running of annual service surveys. This trend involves designing parts of the organisation around customer or market segments or channels rather than around products or technologies (which is more normal). Where some functions cannot be aligned to a particular customer grouping, organisations are designing "front ends" (interface with customer and industry groups) and "back ends" (organised by product or technology). The overall point is that the customer focus is penetrating deeper and deeper into most organisations. "One stop shops", key account structures, empowered service agents and inverted pyramids are general examples of customer-oriented structures.

► SPECIFIC EXAMPLES

LINTAS is a major advertising agency with a world-wide client base. At each of their offices in Asia, LINTAS employ "Account Managers". The role of an Account Manager is to ensure that the clients' needs are fully met by internal agency staff. The Account Manager meets with the client to discuss the initial brief. They subsequently work with the client and the internal agency experts to review the marketing "positioning" (target audience, aim of the campaign, etc.) for the specific project. During the project, they help pull the various internal functions (Art, Media Buying, Creative, etc.) in a common direction, massaging the relationships between these and "running interference" on behalf of the client.

At Sutton Cross, just outside Dublin city, Superquinn hold a number of weekly focus group meetings. Through a series of carefully controlled questions, this format allows the "voice of the customer" to be introduced to the heart of the organisation. The customers do not receive any payment for attending the hour long meetings, other than some refreshments that are made available. The reward is being treated by an organisation in a way which sends a clear signal that "you are important to us", and the evidence of tangible changes in products and services which were the direct result of previous meetings.

Feargal Quinn often personally attends these meetings, reinforcing the importance of the forum. Interestingly, Superquinn also portray the customer in their official organisation chart. In addition they have renamed their Head Office in Sutton as the Support Office, sending a subtle but important message to "staffers" that adding value happens at the coal-face in the retail stores.

KEY STRUCTURAL QUESTIONS

- Is your organisation simple to deal with — from your customers' perspective?

- Do the customers have to deal with several internal people to solve a problem?

- How has the organisation built the "voice of the customer" into products and services?

KEY PRINCIPLE 6:
CLARITY OF ROLES & ACCOUNTABILITY

A key principle of effective organisation design is to avoid overlaps (where two or more people are responsible for the same thing) and underlaps (where no one in an organisation has responsibility for something important). This is achieved through the establishment of clear goals and responsibilities.

While the notion that people in organisations should have clear goals and accountabilities is hardly revolutionary, a lack of goal and role clarity for individuals is a continual feature within client companies. Apart from the obvious fallout in terms of reduced productivity (lack of role clarity often leads to anxiety which in turn leads to lowered productivity), this can have a less visible but equally damaging impact on an organisation in relation to interpersonal conflict.

We often respond to requests for "team building exercises" with an explanation of the GRIP model (an anagram for Goals, Roles, Processes and Interpersonals). Central point: In our experience many of the problems in organisations that are described as "interpersonal conflict" or "team building issues" are often the result of a lack of clarity around Goals, Roles or Processes. The proper design of these segments often helps to alleviate symptoms much more effectively than traditional team building interventions which seek to bolster interpersonal relationships (symptoms) but often do not address the heart of the problem (which can be "structural" as well as "relational").

SPECIFIC EXAMPLE

One company we worked with supplied a range of industrial hygiene products including "pull down" toilet towels. In addition to the person who delivered the towels, the company had two separate customer contact groups — the "sales representatives" (whose job was to increase sales) and the "service representatives" (who dealt with any customer service issues that emerged.

The sales representatives were paid by a bonus system based on the volume of business sold. The service representatives were paid a fixed salary and measured against the level of customer service achieved. Both groups were located separately in the building complex and had no opportunity to formally meet. Because of the separation of their "roles" there were constant conflicts of interest between the groups and continual scapegoating; the personal relationships between the two groups were put at risk by the lack of clarity regarding how their goals should be mutually supportive.

KEY STRUCTURAL QUESTIONS

- Are key result areas (written in output terms) set for all managers?

- Are measurements set against each of these?

- How is performance tracked?

- How are changes in priorities negotiated?

- How are the goals for people in the different departments linked?

- Are there any important goals which do not have an owner?

Consultants who specialise in the area of job evaluation advise that the "minimum" perceivable distance between jobs is 15 per cent. What this means in effect is that small increases in job size are not detectable or measurable. This gives rise to the notion of "distance" in reporting relationships (a concept related to the sizing of individual jobs rather than to any notion of social distance).

Is there a "standard" distance that should be targeted and can be measured? While this is dependent on the nature of the work, there is a theoretical notion that a "one stratum" distance in reporting relationships is technically correct. It is normally "measured" by the type of behaviour exhibited in an organisation.

Reporting relationships of less than one stratum distance are often visible by:

• too much contact time between boss and subordinate

• too many one-over-one decisions

• subordinate (c) bypassing (b) to get to (a)

• (c) saying that (a) is the "real" boss

• (b) keeping his head down and staying out of trouble

• (a) frequently by-passing (b) to get to (c).

Reporting relationships of more than one stratum distance are also problematical, giving rise to a different set of conditions. These are sometimes visible by an "overloaded/underloaded" manager, subordinates feeling that the manager is too "distant", the manager getting impatient with detail and new subordinates feeling pressurised to learn quickly.

▶ SPECIFIC EXAMPLE

In a large financial services company in the UK the behaviour of one of the senior managers was causing difficulty. Firstly, the managers below him complained of being "oversupervised". Secondly, in a time of poor organisational performance this manager extended his personal office. Finally, the manager made a push to become President of the Golf Society by contributing a substantial personal trophy. What caused this behaviour? While many explanations are possible, the core explanation lies in the organisational structure principle of "stratum distance" in job design. This person's job added little value to the managers who reported to him. This was an issue of poor job design, not one of personal capacity. The behaviours exhibited were the outward expression of the manager's own search for a "visible role" in the organisation. The problem was eventually resolved when he took over a substantial portfolio of new developmental work (albeit keeping the bigger office).

▶ KEY STRUCTURAL QUESTIONS

- Are any of the presenting issues listed above a feature of your organisation?

- Does the current job design broadly conform to patterns in similar organisations?

- Are there particular managers or sections which seem to have too little or too much to do?

KEY PRINCIPLE 8:
COST EFFECTIVENESS

Structure should be cost effective; no duplication of functions should exist and all functions must explicitly add value to the organisation's goals. A sub-goal here is that structure should foster synergy, e.g. centralised purchasing. As a general point, the wider the unit of analysis under consideration the greater the scope for cost-effective structural reform.

▶ SPECIFIC EXAMPLES

The first of a series of change programmes at Guinness in Dublin comprised a multiplicity of separate departmental plans; the second of the series took as the unit of analysis the whole brewery, in which case some of the existing structures were eliminated, split, merged and so forth. Later programmes took as the unit of analysis all the breweries in Ireland and the UK, resulting in further savings through structural synergies across several sites.

In Sterling Winthrop Asia, purchasing of the raw material paracetemol was conducted on a plant by plant basis. Paracetemol was shipped from Ireland and the UK to individual plants in Malaysia, Indonesia, the Philippines and Taiwan. Because the lead times were quite long (up to 12 weeks) and the demand for products in the individual countries was difficult to forecast, the plant managers tended to over-order (a "just-in-case" purchasing strategy). The net result was huge stock holding levels and low stock turn — the organisational equivalent of putting savings under the mattress. The establishment of a co-ordinated (not centralised) purchasing system in Asia where materials could be quickly re-routed between countries overcame the problem.

 KEY STRUCTURAL QUESTIONS

- Are any of the key functions duplicated?

- Do any departments/divisions experience "role conflict" due to duplication of roles with other areas?

- When seeking cost savings are you adapting a unit by unit frame of reference or a single, wider "set of brackets"?

KEY PRINCIPLE 9: WIDER SPAN OF CONTROL/ UMBILICAL CORD MANAGEMENT

Seminal work completed by industrial sociologists in the UK and USA attempted to classify organisation types in relation to the particular technology employed. A sub-feature of this work was the notion that there is a predetermined "span of control", an outer limit of people who can be managed directly.

For some years the dominant thinking was that the maximum number of people that can be supervised effectively is about ten. This notion of a limited span of control of less than a dozen people has come to be accepted as a "management truism"; in companies with a greater number of people being managed directly, this is often highlighted as a "structural flaw".

The debate on the effective "span of control" may need to be reopened for two reasons. Firstly, much of the current thinking on empowerment envisages a completely different style of management — one that is much less involved in the minutiae of day-to-day operations (see later points). Secondly, the "less than a dozen" theory ignores the huge potential of information technology which enables much wider spans of control than could have been envisaged a couple of years ago. Relatively recent developments in information technology (e.g. distributed information systems, expert systems, cellular phones, portable computers) have changed the ground rules in organisation structuring.

An important consideration is the diversity of activities reporting into one person; if all the activities are similar, e.g. branches of a bank, then the span can be much wider than if the activities are more heterogeneous.

SPECIFIC EXAMPLE

Janet O' Donnell is Director of Telemarketing for the Right Start Catalogue in the USA, the nation's largest direct mail vendor of baby products. Her work force of up to 170 full and part-time operators answer phones 24 hours a day, seven days a week, from their own homes. While Janet has more scheduling headaches than the typical manager, she is assisted by a piece of software called "PeopleScheduler" from Adaptive Software in California. From her computer monitor, Janet can see each individual's name, title and shift, including their individual breaks. It warns of potential conflicts, updates and moves times around if someone calls in sick and produces statistical summaries of absences and tardiness. Before this particular software was written Janet kept track by using Lotus 1-2-3 which took up to half of her available time just to enter the data. With the new software she can complete this exercise in about half an hour *(Fortune*, May 1994).

KEY STRUCTURAL QUESTIONS

- What are the existing spans of control?

- Are there delays in decision-making which hinder effective functioning?

- Could managers handle wider spans of control if they had better processes and supporting information technology?

KEY PRINCIPLE 10:
VALUE CHAIN INTEGRATION

A key organisational theme in recent times is "boundary management". Traditionally organisations managed one specific step along the value chain. Thus farmers grew barley which in turn was sold to intermediaries and made into malt. Once this stage was completed, the malt was sold on to brewers and distillers as a raw material for alcohol manufacturing. This end product was then sold to wholesalers, retailers and, eventually, to the consumer.

However, the reality of organisations today is often no longer simply what is "inside the walls" of any particular company but encompasses the relationship with other companies along the value chain. Organisation structure should reflect the industry evolution, capitalising on opportunities along the value chain. Marianne DeVanna, Professor of Organisational Behaviour at Columbia University in the USA, wrote of the "boundaryless organisation", a concept which has become most widely associated with the internal processes within General Electric, but now has a much wider application.

▶ **SPECIFIC EXAMPLE**

At Irish Sugar, a subsidiary of Greencore, farmers enter into annual contracts to grow and sell beet to the company. As beet is the second most lucrative farm produce (after milk), the annual contracts are always oversubscribed. Once the sugar has been extracted from the beet the pulp is then re-sold to the farmers for use as animal feed. Greencore, through a range of subsidiary companies, also offer several additional products to farmers (e.g. fertilisers) and this can be traded off against the beet sold. Both the company and the producers are thus locked into a highly beneficial and integrated supply role which normally continues over a long time period, often until the farmer dies.

 KEY STRUCTURAL QUESTIONS

- Where is the organisation placed along the industry value chain?

- Is there opportunity to structurally integrate (forwards or backwards) along the value chain?

- What is the likely industry evolution?

The historical model of the organisation is based on two fundamental principles:

1 **Functional divisions**, with each of the specialist "arms" of an organisation being separate from the rest of the organisation

2 **Specialisation of labour**, with a narrow subdivision of tasks.

Both of the above principles are borrowed from the military model of organisational effectiveness. Functional division was seen to support the specialist nature of the military "branches" (Infantry, Signals, Engineering Corps, Intelligence etc.). Specialism of labour was based on the notion that a military unit attracted "low quality" manpower and the amount of information which could be "downloaded" to each individual was severely limited. The solution was good integration, analogous to a "well-oiled machine" with closely fitting parts. During times of battle, each of the component parts would perform its allotted function without question and by rote. Even where communications were difficult (as in most battle conditions) the military machine would perform as expected.

The appropriateness of an active subdivision of labour as the preferred organisational model for commercial organisations is now being questioned. For example, the principle of self-sufficiency finds expression today in organisational forms such as semi-autonomous work groups, empowerment, stand-alone business units and so forth. These structural forms have great strength in their responsiveness to customers and their motivational value for staff (people like being self-sufficient).

SPECIFIC EXAMPLE

At one large manufacturing company in the South East, the organisational structure maintained a strict division between production and maintenance personnel. If a machine in the production area broke down, the supervisor called his counterpart in maintenance and arranged for a craftsperson to come and resolve the problem.

This structure (which is fairly typical) had two direct results. Firstly, the maintenance of the equipment was seen as an "engineering" issue rather than being the responsibility of production personnel. Secondly, it generated a huge amount of scapegoating between the two sections (maintenance personnel felt that the production operators had little concern about the way in which the machinery was run; production personnel felt that the internal service offered by maintenance was both slow and poor mannered).

THE SOLUTION

The two functions were integrated by having the maintenance people report to a production supervisor. They had a "dotted line" link to an engineering manager (a qualified engineer) who maintained their skill levels and provided a "faculty focus". While this particular solution would not work in all areas (often due to the poor relationships, rather than any technical objection), it does highlight an unnecessary hankering in most current organisation design for the military model of specialisation of labour.

The concept of self-sufficiency means that a department needs to have control over the resources it commonly uses. It does not mean that all of these resources need to be in-house. For example, within Dublin Fire Brigade one Fire Officer in each station looks after the supply and cooking of food for the other officers. Because of the nature of the work and the duration of the shift rosters completed, it is very important that access to hot food is available to this group. However, this could probably be provided much more cost-effectively by sub-contracting this service to a local cook, rather than tying up the services of a highly trained Fire Officer. The concept of self-sufficiency has to be balanced against the (at times contradictory) notion of cost-effectiveness.

▶ KEY STRUCTURAL QUESTIONS

- Is there any duplication of units, specialists or other resources?

- Does a particular department import routinely needed necessities?

- Is there recurring trouble at an organisational interface?

KEY PRINCIPLE 12:
CONSCIOUS DESIGN FOR INNOVATION

Ask most chief executives if innovation and continuous improvement are important in their particular businesses and you will get a resounding "YES". The answer to the follow-on question — "What structures have you set in place to achieve this?" — are often less certain. There is a growing recognition that "innovation" (defined as the constant improvement of existing processes coupled with the generation of radical new ideas) is not something which "just happens"; it needs to be explicitly designed into organisational structures and routines. Essentially, the rhythms of current operations and innovation are different so they need to be structured separately and yet still be linked, e.g. to facilitate new product introduction.

In redesigning the top level structures of two consumer food companies last year, strategic marketing and product architecture — which has to do with spotting and developing new business opportunities — were separated from trade marketing — which has to do with the bustle of promoting the existing portfolio of products. Recent research by McKinsey endorses this separation of the innovative work from the operational. If they are not separated, the innovative agenda is typically driven away by the "gravitational pull" and urgency of the operational focus.

► SPECIFIC EXAMPLE: HARDWARE

General Electric operate a huge "white goods" manu-facturing facility in Lexington, Ohio (the operation employs 16,000 people and the employee car park has traffic lights to control the flows). Overall, the "house-keeping" at the plant conforms to world-class stan-dards. However, in one small corner site there is a building which is separate from the main. This is the "plastics group skunk works" where GE engineers are encouraged to "play" with new concepts and materials. In short, it is an innovation centre which operates to a distinctly different set of norms than the rest of the facility. The first thing one notices upon entering this part of the facility is the seeming chaos — nothing seems to be in any particular order, in marked contrast to the almost military order of the rest of the complex. It is precisely because GE understands that you need to explicitly separate "innovation" from "operating" that they have created this "reservation" for new ideas.

► SPECIFIC EXAMPLE: SOFTWARE

As noted earlier, Bank of Ireland Credit Card Services operate from centre city offices in Dublin. Just over 120 people are employed. As part of their Customer Services programme they ran a specific ideas generation session (what can be thought of as a "shake the tree" event). The result: 120 people managed to generate over 4,000 suggestions for improvement, an astonishing number of ideas per individual in a single session. It confirms the belief that most people are "oil gushers" of creativity; good process design allows this resource to be tapped.

KEY PRINCIPLE 13:
EFFECTIVE "WORK-BETWEEN-THE-BOXES"

Many organisations are "stove piped" with most work structured according to defined "functions". A general principle is that the more differentiated an organisation is in terms of functional specialism, the more difficult it is to integrate these. Thus in the pharmaceutical industry specific efforts have to be made to integrate the work of the research chemists, the marketers and the financial personnel (who often, quite happily, work totally independently of each other). In so many organisations there is a "win-lose" mentality between departments; in the worst cases they seem to be working to an operating principle of "survival of the fittest".

It follows that there is a specific organisation need for lateral/horizontal linking mechanisms between operating groups. In practice this can be achieved in a number of different ways (interlinking the objectives through some form of "team-based" objectives setting, it can be a specific part of the role of some individuals — "an integrating/liaison role" — or it can be managed through task forces, meetings, standing committees, matrix management structures or other forms of prescribed contact).

The actual methods employed to co-ordinate the relationships between functions will depend on the nature of the particular tasks. Co-ordination through standardisation works well in stable environments (e.g. McDonald's). Co-ordination by plan works well in less stable environments (e.g. building a new office block) whereas co-ordination by mutual adjustment allows continuous feedback in volatile environments (e.g. a consulting company running an organisational change project). The general principle is that a fixed hierarchy tends to work in more stable environments; where the environment is less stable, the organisational design needs to be more fluid (often referred to as "organic") to cater for this.

 KEY STRUCTURAL QUESTIONS

- How well do the current sections of the organisation work together?

- To what degree are the functions in the organisation mutually dependent?

- What existing opportunities exist to improve "work between the boxes"?

KEY PRINCIPLE 14: DECISION-MAKING AT THE APPROPRIATE POINT/DELEGATION

A central principle of effective organisation design is that decision-making responsibility should be located at the appropriate point in the organisation. The current term for this concept is "empowerment". Unfortunately, too much of the debate around the concept of empowerment centres on the concept as a "social good" and too little on its performance improvement impact.

"SIMULTANEOUS LOOSE/TIGHT PROPERTIES"

Some would argue that empowerment works better in some industries than others. For example, in the pharmaceutical industry there is little scope for divergence when making up a batch of tablets. No company wants the employees to "try" a new recipe or to mix the ingredients in a different order. Similarly, McDonald's want employees to fry Big Macs for a precise duration; there are no "rare" or "well done" burger options and no innovation is required or allowed in the cooking process (at McDonald's the procedures on cooking and cleaning are completely prescribed in a 700 page book).

A key point is that empowerment needs to be bounded while, at the same time, allowing some degree of autonomy and personal expression. The idea here is for an organisation to develop "simultaneous loose/tight properties", a concept first espoused in the best-selling book *In Search of Excellence*. Thus while McDonald's burgers in Orchard Road, Singapore taste exactly the same as burgers from McDonald's, O'Connell Street in Dublin, the person serving the burger is likely to be a pensioner in Singapore and a student in Dublin. There are a whole range of initiatives which can be decided "locally" in relation to marketing, staffing etc.

Key Point: The "centre" of the doughnut needs to be carefully managed but there are huge degrees of freedom around this. Even in very tightly controlled processes, empowerment can work well once the concept that "not everything is on the agenda" is understood and accepted.

Another way to express this balance is to say that "you have to centralise in order to decentralise"; you can only delegate, empower, decentralise effectively when you have good systems, good training, good audit disciplines and so forth in place.

▶ SPECIFIC EXAMPLES

A large Irish food manufacturer and distributor decentralised its purchasing activity to various departments — materials, engineering, marketing, transport — because the centralised processes were felt to be too bureaucratic. Two years later they reversed this decision by re-centralising, because there was a lack of discipline in the dispersed purchasing. What was missing when they decentralised was the necessary set of basic systems, procedures and training to which the decentralised purchasers would adhere while otherwise exercising their own discretion.

In one long-established company in the South East, promotion was widely used as a reward mechanism by the department managers with little involvement of the Personnel Department. The cumulative effect over time was an enormously costly managerial cohort. This kind of structural drift happened imperceptibly but lead to a labour cost band which was grossly uncompetitive and eventually had to be addressed through radical downsizing and outplacement.

 ## KEY STRUCTURAL QUESTIONS

- Is there a slowness of response time in decision-making?

- Does the company often experience implementation delays?

- Do people consider the organisation to be too bureaucratic or centralised?

- When is the last time that the concept of "decision-controls" was discussed by the management team?

KEY PRINCIPLE 15:
FLATTENING HIERARCHY

There is a definite world-wide trend towards the delayering of organisations. An issue of *Personnel Management* in the UK even noted that the military were currently conducting a review of the historical command-and-control structures to decide if these were still appropriate in a modern army! It is also interesting that the Catholic Church, a major multinational organisation, has essentially five layers between the local priest and the Pope, while a Wexford-based plant with 300 employees had seven in the managerial hierarchy. In many commercial organisations, middle managers are an endangered species.

Flatter organisation structures have a number of potential advantages. Firstly, they provide a speedier mechanism for making decisions (they have less internal layers). As knowledge in an organisation often resides at the "coalface"; if all decisions are taken at the next level up this slows down the process. Secondly, it tends to promote ownership of decisions. The first law of psychology is that people do not resist their own ideas; flatter organisational structures support this principle by pushing the decision-taking responsibility downwards.

The use of information technology can also make a real difference in this area. For example, the use of Lotus Notes and e-mail at one electronics engineering plant in Cork effectively meant that everyone in the plant who worked at a desk was linked into a common communications system. As information was historically the "pass key" for position in organisation, a tangible difference in organisational levels and corresponding status has effectively disappeared.

▶ SPECIFIC EXAMPLE

Pakistan Railways is a large (130,000 employees) state railway organisation with responsibility for operating the railways throughout that vast country. The railway structures, established by the British when they controlled the territory, are based on the military model. Currently there are an incredible 23 levels in the structure between the General Manager and the lowest ranks (who have the official title "peons"). In contrast, at An Post (7,000 + employees) part of a recent mandate is that there cannot be more than 5 levels in the organisation from Chief Executive to the most junior postal operative (Hynes, 1994).

There have been numerous Irish examples of de-layering in recent years including Guinness, Irish Life and Pepsi. It is a trend that most likely will be with us for some time to come. In the near term future, tall organisation structures are destined to become the dinosaurs of the commercial world.

▶ KEY STRUCTURAL QUESTIONS

- How many levels are in the existing organisation?
- Is there visible added value provided by each level?
- Does referral of items occur that could be handled laterally at lower levels?

KEY PRINCIPLE 16:
CENTRES OF EXCELLENCE

Many multinationals are evolving from "command-and-control" structures to networks of "centres of excellence". In this new scenario the centre should add distinctive value and not necessarily house functions which have a corporate-wide role, e.g. IT or management development.

▶ SPECIFIC EXAMPLE

Ford Motor Company needed to invest three billion dollars to design the car line for Taurus and Sable, two USA brands. The company could not afford to spend another three billion investment for Europe and overcame this problem by designing the products to satisfy both markets from the outset with appropriate design modifications. In this particular case (and very much throughout the multinational sector), the headquarters of organisations are being distributed around the world to where the competence exists to perform a particular function or responsibility. These organisations are held together less by formal authority and more by mutual dependency and shared values. The emerging telecommunications networks (e.g. video conferencing) make this concept eminently practical.

In passing, it is perhaps worth noting that this trend presents an opportunity to Irish subsidiaries of multinationals to become the "centre of excellence" worldwide for a particular skill, function or product.

KEY STRUCTURAL QUESTIONS

- How centralised are the current organisational functions?

- Are there any activities which would more appropriately be performed in the field than in HQ?

- How would your site bid to become the "centre of excellence" for a particular competency?

Another world-wide trend is the movement towards the so-called "modular corporation". The essence of this design revolves around sub-contracting and the leveraging of core competencies. The key organisational task is deciding which activities are to be performed inside the organisation and which are to be purchased externally. Hollowing-out can also be considered in a second way — the movement to the so-called "Smiley-Curve". Traditionally the bulk of labour was employed in manufacturing. Given the increasing mechanisation of the production process, the amount of labour consumed in the production process is minimal and this is moving both to the left and right of the manufacturing cycle (that is, to research and customer services respectively).

SPECIFIC EXAMPLES

Benetton has only a handful of stores in key retail markets which are used to gauge customer response information and to innovate in merchandising. Virtually no sales, design or manufacturing operations are conducted directly by the company. All of these operations are performed by sub-contractors, franchisees and free-lance designers. Benetton is responsible for the marketing of all products, through a large staffing of product managers, and they also control the information and logistical systems which allow this diverse group to be co-ordinated. Essentially the only assets managed by this huge group is intellectual capital.

Digital Software in Galway used to reproduce most of their manuals for distribution throughout Europe. Now they manage relationships with a network of printers who complete the actual production of these.

 KEY STRUCTURAL QUESTIONS

- Could you subcontract out any of your existing functions?

- Have you any vital, unique skills that you could leverage (exploit) through the multiplier effect of collaborating or franchising?

- Have you conducted a "make/buy" analysis of existing products or functions?

KEY PRINCIPLE 18: COARSE-GRAINED VS FINE-GRAINED GRADING STRUCTURES

Frederick Winslow Taylor is the father of the concept of job design. Under what has become popularly known as "Taylorism", people were to perform narrowly defined jobs. Thus workers in car manufacturing plants were individually responsible for very narrow pieces of work. Even where jobs were seen to be more varied (e.g. craftsmen) people simply moved further along a particular vertical specialism. In recent times the concept of job design has undergone some radical shifts in thinking. From the pioneering work of Frederick Hertzberg in the 1960s the twin concepts of "job enrichment" and "job enlargement" emerged.

The move to "coarse-grained" grading structures represents an emerging trend. In part it is a recognition that employment is becoming much more knowledge-intensive and the need for redesigned jobs potentially provides a range of organisational and individual benefits. Through "job enlargement" (defined as adding "extra bits" into a job) and "job enrichment" (vertical integration which often includes elements of planning/control) people are being asked to be more flexible in their contribution to organisations and are being given more autonomy/self-control in return. In most cases a "cradle to grave" sense of responsibility has a positive effect on decreasing boredom and making jobs more meaningful for individuals.

One argument against this trend is that some jobs (depending on the technology employed/industry) do not lend themselves to enrichment. For example, one of the key jobs in the industrial hygiene company referred to earlier was to search the pockets of incoming work overalls prior to the laundering process (just as most people search shirt pockets in the domestic environment prior to washing). Coats from butchers shops, garages and various other users of industrial workwear produced a variety of objects including dead mice (quite common), razor blades (which often injured the hands of the workers searching the pockets) and all sorts of personal paraphernalia. Can such jobs be enriched? One way is to do the planning and actual work in teams rather than on an individual basis. In this way the "process" as distinct from the job "content" becomes enriched.

SPECIFIC EXAMPLE

Proctor and Gamble has introduced what they call their "technician concept", an employee who over the course of several years masters all of the core manufacturing processes and also develops a basic understanding of support functions such as maintenance, quality control, finance and information technology. The benefit to the individual is more autonomy, more interesting work and more income; the company achieve greater labour utilisation, less turnover and higher productivity.

KEY STRUCTURAL QUESTIONS

- To what extent are the full skills and abilities of people within the organisation utilised?

- Have you ever consciously looked at the area of job design to see if this could be improved?

KEY PRINCIPLE 19: LEARNING/ CONTINUOUS IMPROVEMENT ROUTINES

Within organisations there is often a gap between what people say "should" happen (in terms of planning and forecasting) and what actually happens. In many cases no one talks about this difference and organisations which experience the inconsistency simply roll forward. Some organisations have now consciously designed "learning routines" into their structure as a way of understanding and learning from their environment. "Organisational learning" can be defined as the "ability of an organisation to detect and correct an error in its functioning". It is a relatively new term for a process which well-managed organisations have had in place for some time.

Organisations need to separate the operational ("how many computers did we ship yesterday?") from the strategic ("do we want to be in this part of the industry?") issues. By trying to manage both agendas in the same forum, e.g. the weekly management meeting, inevitably the strategic issues get pushed aside. As one wry manager recently noted: "In (Company X) the urgent pushes out the important".

One academic (Chris Argyris) has distinguished between what he termed "single loop" and "double loop" learning.

Single Loop Learning: Organisations can detect errors in functions. This makes them more effective in what they are doing. Typically it involves changing things (rather than the basic policies, objectives or philosophies).

Double Loop Learning: Organisations not only detect errors in the way things are done, but also question the basic principles. Most organisations are not good at double loop learning and can sometimes go to great lengths to avoid reviews in this area as it challenges the status quo.

▶ SPECIFIC EXAMPLE

Organisational learning can be driven in a number of different ways. At the Royal Dutch Shell Company, one of the methods used is the creation of "microworlds". These are future scenarios based on a range of possibilities ("What will be our response if the price of oil jumps to $50 per barrel/falls to $10 per barrel? What *was* our response the last time we had a major price fluctuation?").

▶ KEY STRUCTURAL QUESTIONS

- Does the organisation take "time out" to review events in detail?

- What formal mechanisms exist to "build in obselescence" to management routines?

- Do you set specific "continuous improvement" targets?

KEY PRINCIPLE 20:
ORGANISATIONAL ALIGNMENT

The final point under our "Top 20" listing of organisation design principles is that of alignment. Structure must be aligned with the other elements in the organisation. A useful checklist is provided by the McKinsey 7S framework of organisational elements (Strategy, Structure, Skills, Systems, Staffing, Style and Superordinate Goals).

▶ SPECIFIC EXAMPLES

One of the large building societies in Ireland has a stated goal of promoting "teamwork" throughout the organisation. The benefits of teamwork, as extolled by this company, are as follows:

1 The sharing of "best practises" throughout the group

2 The promotion of a climate of co-operation.

However the reward system in the company for branch managers is based on a league table of specific issues which cover both business growth and profitability. Not surprisingly, the level of teamwork between the branches is less than optimum and the company are somewhat disappointed with the results of the teamwork implementation programme to date (the folly of rewarding "A" while hoping for "B"). In many organisations new processes are often needed (e.g. Performance Appraisal for teams) to support the stated philosophy.

Another financial services company declared that its key competitive/strategic weapon would be customer service. But structurally the Customer Service Manager remained in a middle management role responsible for the "back office". There were no measurement systems to track customer service performance, and the databases of the organisation were cut by product and not by customer.

Central Point: Non-alignment of structure and other elements is all too commonplace in organisational design.

KEY STRUCTURAL QUESTIONS

- To what extent are the various parts of the organisation "aligned"?

- Are there any obvious disconnects between the different organisational elements (pay systems, managerial behaviour, appraisal, planning, use of space etc.)?

CONCLUSION

In this chapter we have attempted to set out the major design principles underlying the construction of a high performance organisation. If a management team invests effort in understanding the impact of structure on its operations there will often be some current elements missing or some structural inconsistencies, particularly if the existing structure has been in place for some time. Structures are strongly conservative in the sense of tending to perpetuate themselves.

If this effort is extended into crafting an "architect's impression" of the future, there will usually be a number of new structural elements needed. Unless these discontinuities in structure (to manage today effectively and to plan for tomorrow) are deliberately managed, the existing structure will tend to perpetuate itself far beyond its usefulness and the desired new structures will not be developed soon enough.

It follows that it is imperative periodically to question all organisational structures (both reporting relationships and the interlinking processes which bind these together). While the timing on this will differ from industry to industry, it is unlikely if any particular structural configuration would maintain its shelf life for longer than a couple of years.

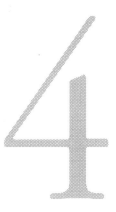

PERFORMANCE
PLANNING

4.1 FOCUSED PERFORMANCE MANAGEMENT: INTRODUCTION

The first faults are theirs that commit them; the second theirs that permit them

Anon

Managing employee performance is a critical element in ensuring organisational success. In companies where an effective performance management system is in place, employees work towards clearly defined goals and receive performance feedback on an ongoing basis. The best systems are directly linked to the organisation's strategic business plans and highlight the contribution that each employee makes towards these. Everyone knows their "role in the show".

The following three chapters have been designed to allow you to benchmark your existing Performance Management System against best practices in leading edge organisations. They highlight the three core elements of any well functioning performance management system:

1 Performance Planning

2 Performance Coaching

3 Performance Review.

This particular chapter focuses on the first element of a focused performance management system, Performance Planning, which takes place at the start of the performance cycle. A model of the overall system is outlined on the following page.

FIGURE 1
The Performance Management System

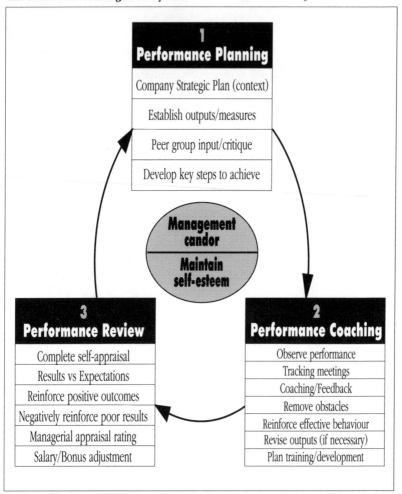

PERFORMANCE MANAGEMENT: WHY BOTHER?

An effective performance management system is a critical requirement in instilling a high performance culture within a company. Four specific reasons support this assertion:

▶ PERFORMANCE MANAGEMENT: THE CENTRE OF THE HUMAN RESOURCE WHEEL

Performance management is the *key* organisational variable. No other human resources system has as much impact on the success of an organisation. For any company to be successful in the longer term, it must engender a high performance culture.

The Lesson: In large organisations a formal system to manage performance is required.

▶ LESSONS FROM THE EXCELLENT COMPANIES

In recent years there have been a number of separate studies of "excellence". The "excellent" companies are initially selected on the basis of *business results*, i.e. they exhibited high performance in financial terms. This led researchers to study why these companies have been so successful. A central element in their success was a system designed to set performance objectives and to track performance results.

The Lesson: A formal system to manage performance is a key element in the management apparatus of those companies we admire most.

Performance Planning as explained in this chapter is based on the best ideas/systems within several excellent companies operating in Ireland and internationally.

THE ICEBERG FACTOR

In many companies, employees operate at less than their full potential. An effective performance management system can deliver the missing percentage for free! It can deliver more work time and more effective use of the currently available work time.

COMPETENCE AND COMMITMENT: THE TWO Cs OF PERFORMANCE

Everybody talks about the weather, but nobody does anything about it

Charles Dudley Warner

Two issues impact performance — competence and commitment. Think about it. Highly competent (skilled) people committed to their objectives — that is what we are aiming for.

The Lesson: Performance Planning as explained in this chapter will have a positive impact on both competence and commitment. It sends a clear signal to employees with regard to expected work performance (company commitment), gets the employees involved in the planning process (employee commitment) and assesses their training/development needs (employee competence).

Performance planning is a way to ensure that everyone in the business has a clear set of "goalposts". Specifically:

When we try to pick out anything by itself, we find it hitched to everything else in the universe

John Muir

1 It translates a company's strategic business plans into concrete action plans at every level within the organisation. The intent is to have a "seamless garment" between strategic planning and the action plans of each individual within the company.

2 It sets clear and realistic "goalposts", focusing individuals on 6-8 outputs (results) which the company expects them to produce within a 12 month period.[1]

3 It allows an employee to have an input into the goals being set for the other members of their work team. Through a joint goal-setting meeting, every member of the team has a better understanding of the goals of their fellow team members. This has the potential to significantly improve teamworking throughout the company.

4 It sets out clear measurements (the standard of performance expected for each output area) so people know in advance the specific criteria against which they will be assessed at their performance review.

---

1 In some organisations where the rate of change/flux is particularly rapid, this planning period can be reduced to as little as three-month time spans.

5 It has an in-built mechanism to track performance each quarter between the manager and individual employee.

6 It provides a direct link between performance and the reward system.

7 It highlights the training and development needs of individuals.

Overall the system is designed to promote candour in the relationship and to improve the performance and self-esteem of the people in the organisation.

ONE BEST WAY?

There is no "one best way" to manage performance which will suit all organisations. The central ideas in this chapter need to be customised to meet the needs of individual organisations and, in some cases, can be "bolted on" to the existing performance management formats.

▶ WHAT ARE KEY RESULT AREAS?

Key Result Areas are the specific areas of achievement which are critically important to the successful completion of a job. They represent the reason why a particular job exists.

▶ WHAT ARE OUTPUTS?

Outputs are products or services produced as part of the job.[2] Some outputs are directly provided to external customers, e.g. a pension product that is sold. Some outputs are passed on to the next person in the work process, e.g. a marketing report which is submitted to another department. Outputs (often labelled as Key Result Areas) depend on the particular role in the organisation. When written outputs emphasise completed work, they convey a sense of purpose and accomplishment.

▶ WHAT ARE INPUTS?

Inputs are what are used to produce an output or end result. Over the course of a day, week or month several activities may be performed which contribute to

---

2 Much of the pioneering work on outputs was completed by the Canadian management consultant Bill Reddin in his seminal work 'The Output Oriented Organisation'.

the accomplishment of a single output. While inputs are required to achieve end results, they are not an end in themselves.

WHAT IS MANAGEMENT EFFECTIVENESS?

Effectiveness in the job is determined by the extent to which the output requirements of the position are achieved.

Common difficulties in large companies include:

• Losing sight of the goal

• Losing sight of the bottom line

• People not knowing how their position contributes to the company's strategic objectives.

Companies therefore have to work hard to clarify each person's role.

Until we define Key Result Areas/Outputs we are unable to determine the unique contribution of each person and their level of effectiveness.

WHY IS THE CONCEPT OF
KEY RESULT AREAS/OUTPUTS IMPORTANT?

Performance,

not personality,

determines

effectiveness

Establishing Key Result Areas allows people to focus on the reason why their particular job exists. While inputs (attending meetings, developing reports etc.) can be important sub-steps, successful organisations help people to focus on the specific results which are required in the performance of their role.

The concept of outputs is critically important for organisational success because results pay the bills.

Management effectiveness is not an aspect of personality. Effectiveness is best seen as something a person produces from a situation by managing it appropriately. It represents output not input. It is not so much what managers or staff do (i.e. how they spend their time), but what they achieve.

THREE TYPES OF EFFECTIVENESS

Management effectiveness can be clearly understood when managers learn to distinguish between:

1 Personal Effectiveness

2 Apparent Effectiveness

3 Managerial Effectiveness

These three concepts are quite different from each other.

1. PERSONAL EFFECTIVENESS

Poorly defined jobs can lead to what is called personal effectiveness. Personal effectiveness is defined as "the extent to which a manager achieves their own private objectives". Under this heading the manager is satisfying personal objectives rather that the objectives of the organisation.

In many cases the personal effectiveness objective is aimed at improving the power and prestige of the position or the person (to have more clout, a bigger office, etc.). Ambitious people in an organisation which has few clearly defined Key Results/Outputs are likely to satisfy personal objectives rather than the objectives of the organisation.

2. APPARENT EFFECTIVENESS

*Things are sel-
dom what they
seem; skim milk
masquerades as
cream*

W. S. Gilbert

Apparent effectiveness is defined as "the extent to which a manager gives the appearance of being effective". It is difficult, if not impossible, to judge managerial effectiveness simply by observation of behaviour. Yet managers are often judged as effective or ineffective based on such characteristics as:

- is usually on time

- answers questions/queries promptly

- makes quick decisions

- is good at public relations

- makes great presentations

- works late.[3]

Any behaviour must be evaluated only in terms of whether or not it is appropriate to the real needs of the job. The qualities above may be important in some jobs and situations and in others may be much less relevant to effectiveness.

3. MANAGERIAL EFFECTIVENESS

Managerial effectiveness is defined as "the extent to which an individual achieves the output requirements of their position". The first step in helping managers to be more effective is to help them to see their job in output terms: "What does my company want me to achieve?"

---

3 In one organisation a manager defined internal success as "the ability to have your office light on a timer to make it appear that you always work late".

INPUTS vs OUTPUTS

The difference between inputs and outputs in a work context is illustrated by the following examples:

Effective man-
agers think in
terms of outputs
rather than
inputs

Inputs	Outputs
Machine maintenance	Machine availability
Change attitude	Change behaviour
Speed reading	Speed learning [4]
Calls made	Sales made
Training	Fitness

TYPICAL OUTPUTS FOR A SALES MANAGER
1   Sales levels
2   New sales policy
3   Sales costs
4   Line profitability
5   Sales representatives training
6   Updated forecasting system

TYPICAL OUTPUTS FOR A PRODUCTION MANAGER
1   Production level
2   Delivery times
3   Cost levels
4   Quality level
5   Inventory control
6   Machine utilisation

TYPICAL OUTPUTS FOR A BANK TELLER
1   Customer satisfaction
2   Balanced transactions
3   Business development
4   Foreign exchange transactions

---

4 Woody Allen said that he took up speed reading. He then read War and Peace in 4.5 minutes with the comment: "It's about Russia".

EXAMPLES OF KEY RESULTS/OUTPUTS FROM A FINANCIAL SERVICES COMPANY

▶ MARKETING MANAGER

KEY RESULTS IN SUPPORT OF BUSINESS PLAN

1. Strategic Planning

Develop a Strategic Plan for the company which integrates the three distribution channels (brokers, corporate, branches).

Weighting 25%.

2. Annual Operating Plan

Construct a business plan for all products offered by this company. This includes the allocation of resources and the individual product mix, sponsorships and sales incentives plan.

Weighting 20%.

3. Product Development/Implementation

Pre/post launch design and support of all new products.

Weighting 10%.

4. Business Growth/Profitability

Achieve the business growth/profitability targets.

Weighting 30%.

5. Corporate Identity

Strengthen corporate identity in the marketplace.

Weighting 5%

6. Staff Effectiveness

Maximise the productive commitment from the marketing team.

Weighting 10%.

PRODUCT DEVELOPMENT MANAGER

KEY RESULTS IN SUPPORT OF BUSINESS PLAN

1. Product Design

Ensure that each product is financially engineered to allow it to be sold at the lowest possible cost.

Weighting 30%.

2. New Product Implementation

Design and implement flawless delivery plan for all new products across the three product channels.

Weighting 20%.

3. Product Pricing

Determine the price of individual products, choosing from a range of alternatives.

Weighting 10%.

4. Product Development Process

Re-engineer the product development launch process.

Weighting 10%.

5. Laptop Software Development

Specify the software to be used by all sales personnel.

Weighting 20%.

6. Staff Effectiveness

Maximise the productive commitment from the marketing development team.

Weighting 10%.

In addition to confusing an output with an input, errors can occur in defining outputs by erroneously including in, or excluding from, the definition the following four areas:

1 A worry area

2 Another's area

3 A non-measurable area

4 A time area.

 WORRY AREA

An effectiveness area a manager shows as their own because they do not expect the manager whose responsibility it is to deal with it effectively.

It is common in organisations with weak management for the top person to include several "worry areas" among their Key Results/Outputs. A situation that could give rise to a worry area would be a fear about subordinate incompetence.

Example: A marketing person might worry about lost production and the resulting shortfall in the supply of product but this is not part of their output area.

ANOTHER'S AREA

An effectiveness area which a manager shows as their own, over which they have no control

A further error that can arise in defining outputs results from what is called "another's area". This is not to be confused with a worry area in that it arises from a confusion of where the authority lies rather than a fear about subordinate incompetence.

Example: In marketing-oriented firms it is quite common to see decision-making move upward with the successful manager as they get promoted. The manager who replaced the manager promoted might think they have the same effectiveness areas and authority but in fact may not.

Another common problem is that outputs should represent what you do, not what you're responsible for directing others to do. For example, a sales manager would not list products sold during a particular promotion as their output. That is the output of the sales representative. The supervisor of an assembly line would not list widgets assembled as part of their outputs.

NON-MEASURABLE AREA

An effectiveness area whose associated performance standard is difficult to measure

The third error that can occur in writing outputs results from the "non-measurable area". In certain areas it is difficult to measure output. "Communication" and "liaison" are examples of hard to measure outputs.

It is difficult for some managers to accept the principle that accurate measurement is central to performance effectiveness and "if you cannot measure it forget it, as no one will know anyway".

Measurement for some areas may not at first be obvi-

We judge others according to results, how else? Not knowing the process by which results are arrived at

George Eliot

ous but sometimes a measurement method may be found by changing the wording of the effectiveness area. As you become more familiar with the Performance Management System, your ability to accurately define and measure outputs will increase.

 TIME AREA

An item on which a manager spends time but which is not an effectiveness area

A fourth common error that occurs in writing outputs relates to the "time area". It is usually found in a situation of poor organisational design where responsibilities are unclear, a job is too small or a manager is doing something simply because they like to.

Proper use of time can be established by developing a time budget, which consists of allocating a time percentage to each proposed effectiveness area and then ensuring that one (broadly) stays within the parameters set.

CONSTRUCTING
KEY RESULT AREAS/OUTPUTS [5]

> ## HOW DO YOU DECIDE WHAT THE KEY RESULT AREAS/OUTPUTS SHOULD BE?

Below is a sample listing of questions for managers to help develop an initial listing of Key Result Areas/Outputs for their positions. There is some overlap in the questions as they essentially all ask "what is the core purpose of this job and how does this relate to the strategic objectives of the company?"

> ## USEFUL QUESTIONS IN ESTABLISHING KEY RESULT AREAS/OUTPUTS

Review your contribution to your company under the strategic, operational and personal headings

1. STRATEGIC FOCUS:

• What are the strategic goals for my department and how can I contribute to their attainment?

• What is the position's unique contribution to achieving our strategic objectives?

• Are there any themes/emphasis from senior management which I should focus on in the next 12 months (e.g. cost containment, customer service)?

---

5 An exercise to help develop skills in this area is detailed in Appendix D.

2. OPERATIONAL FOCUS:

- Are there significant current or recent problems which I need to focus on/correct?

3. PERSONAL FOCUS:

- Why is my position needed?

- What will change if I am highly effective in the position?

- How would I know with no one telling me when I am performing effectively?

- What authority does the position really have?

- How do I currently spend my time?

- How should I spend my time?

► TESTING YOUR KEY RESULT AREAS/OUTPUTS

Key Result Areas/Outputs, when constructed, should meet the following criteria:

- Represent output not input.

- Be measurable.

- Be an important part of the position.

- Be within the actual limits of authority and responsibility.

- Represent 100 per cent of the outputs of the position.

- Not be so many as to avoid dealing with the essence of the job or so few as to make planning difficult (somewhere between 4-8 is about right).

- Avoid overlaps — where two people are responsible for the same area).

- Avoid underlaps — where no one is responsible for an important area.

The leader is the servant of his followers in that he removes the obstacles that prevent them from doing their jobs. In short, the true leader enables his or her followers to realise their full potential

Max dePree

Some companies establish common outputs which are applicable to all managers (e.g. a common output of staff effectiveness can apply to all managers who have people reporting to them).

The thinking behind this is that each manager recognises that they are partly responsible for the level of effectiveness of their subordinates. The manager will, for example, have to use skill in coaching to ensure that the company gets the full benefit of a highly competent and committed workforce.

In other companies, standard outputs are listed for all managers as a way to help the company move forward along a common path. In one company, for example, four "across the board" outputs were set (increasing sales, customer service, reducing risk and removing cost). All managers had to report their Key Objectives under four headings (the thinking being that if they were not contributing to these objectives, "what were they doing?").

In another example, a manufacturing plant established eight key goals and tasked all managers in the business with developing their key result areas under four or five of the headings (not all managers reported under each heading, e.g. some would only report under four or five of the headings but the entire eight headings were covered by the total management team).

DEFINING PERFORMANCE MEASURES

▶ MEASURING OUTPUTS

Outputs must be measurable and for each output there is normally one or more measurement methods which can be applied to it.

You should

expect what you

inspect

Edward Demming

Performance measures usually fall into five categories:

1 **Quality** (e.g. how well, errors, accuracy). It is performance against a stated quality control standard — a telephone answering time, customer waiting time, queue length, overbooking, the level of customer complaints.

2 **Quantity** (e.g. how much, volume, efficiency). It is based on a "hard number", e.g. revenue earned, passengers carried, production achieved etc.

3 **Timeliness** (e.g. by when, promptness). It is performance within a stated time, by a given deadline or series of deadlines.

4 **Cost** (within stated costs). It is performance within budget, with given staff numbers, with/without overtime etc.

5 **Acceptability** (a report — or a percentage of the recommendations within it — to be implemented or to be acceptable to your boss). This can be a useful measure for "staff" positions where people feel that they are paid for what they know rather than what they achieve.

► SALES OUTPUT

MEASUREMENT EXAMPLE

- Unit sales for territory
- Sales increase of product A
- Number of sales to new customers.

► SETTING PERFORMANCE STANDARDS

All performance standards must be written with time limits and, where possible, with numerical values attached.

Example: Increase sales of product A by £150,000 for period January 1 to December 31.

► SET "STRETCH" TARGETS — BUT NOT TOO HIGH

Targets set should be realistic — a stretch but attainable. Unrealistic expectations lead to frustration and discouragement.

► PERFORMANCE MEASURES: EXAMPLES FROM A FINANCIAL SERVICES COMPANY

MARKETING MANAGER

1 Strategic Planning
- Rolling 3 year strategic plan, approved by the management board, in place by April.
- Approved plan update in place by October.

2 Annual Operating Plan
- Annual operating plan (marketing) developed and approved by the management board by January.

- Three quarterly updates developed and approved.

- Maintain budget conformance (marketing section).

3 Product Development/Implementation
- Six new products priced/launched/in place by October.

- Fully meet all time/budget deadlines as detailed in the individual product launch plan.

4 Business Growth/Profitability
- 48 per cent share of market achieved by mid-year. Position held by end-of-year.

- Achieve budgeted sales figures of £20 million.

- Profitability of new business of £10 million by end-of-year.

5 Corporate Identity
- All action steps in the corporate identity programme to be completed by July.

6 Staff Effectiveness
- Each person will reach "achieved expectations" rating by December.

- Internal customer service feedback will indicate high level of satisfaction with marketing group.

- Individual development plans prepared for all direct reports by August.

PRODUCTS DEVELOPMENTS MANAGER

1 Product Design
- Offer products at the cheapest rate in the marketplace.

- For same product features have the ability to offer the product at a lower cost to the customers. Alternatively offer a range of added features for the same price.

2 New Product Implementation
- IT/Operational systems fully in place for all new products by May.

- Achieve excellent internal customer feedback rating on the quality of plans produced (IT and Business Operations Division) by September.

- New project management process installed by June to manage introductions (time, budgets, etc.).

3 Product Pricing
- Corporate actuary satisfied with professional responsibility re: pricing.

- Pricing of each product to deliver profitability.

4 Product Development Process
- New system designed/agreed with all internal parties by March.

- New system to have the shortest lead-time for product development and launch of any financial services company in Ireland.

5 Laptop Software Development
- Software agreed by March.

- 100 per cent of implementation deadlines met.

6 Staff Effectiveness
- Each person to reach "achieved expectations" rating by end-of-year.

- Individual development: 40 hours off-the-job technical skills training by August.

SETTING OUTPUTS AND
PERFORMANCE STANDARDS: SUMMARY

1 People feel more committed to objectives when they have been personally involved in setting them. Objectives should be jointly agreed by the manager and their direct reports and should dovetail with the strategic plans.

2 Key Results Areas/outputs must emphasise results, not activities.

3 Key Results Areas/outputs should be clear and unambiguous (written and signed by both parties).

4 Individuals should normally direct their efforts to achieving up to six to eight outputs.

5 Outputs must be measurable. This will show the basis on which the subordinate will be appraised at the performance review.

6 Outputs should be ranked in order of priority to ensure that individuals direct their efforts to the "big hitters". To ensure this, each output should be given a relevant weighting.

7 The format has scope to factor in additional work projects that surface during the period. N.B.: Objectives should remain current throughout the year.

PEER INPUT INTO
GOAL SETTING/TRACKING

The greatest opportunities for performance improvement often lie in the functional interfaces – those points at which the baton is being passed from one department to another

A key organisational objective within the company is to encourage and promote teamwork. The Performance Management System provides structure for this vision.

By using the peer input method at the goal-setting stage we ensure that the outputs of everyone in the organisation are aligned vertically and horizontally, meshing objectives. The likelihood of overlap (two or more people responsible for the same output) or underlap (an important output which no one has responsibility for) is significantly reduced.

HOW WILL INDIVIDUAL OUTPUTS/PERFORMANCE MEASURES BE TRACKED?

Progress against outputs set will be tracked in two ways. Firstly, on a regular basis, each individual will give a "status update" to their peer group at a management meeting. Specific time will be set aside for this purpose and these tracking meetings will become a key element of the overall Performance Management System.

Secondly, during the year there will be two interim performance reviews. Here the individual and the manager meet on a one-to-one basis to discuss performance progress during the preceding period.

The outcome of this meeting is recorded on the Performance Management Form and will influence the rating of the person at the end of the review period.

ENSURING CROSS-FUNCTIONAL STITCHING OF INDIVIDUAL OUTPUTS: THE METHOD

Increasingly, "work-between-the-boxes" is becoming ever more important in organisations. A traditional weakness in objectives-setting was the encouragement of department objectives which were contradictory rather than complementary. We have used the following process as a way to overcome this.[6]

▶ HOW WILL INDIVIDUAL OUTPUTS/PERFORMANCE MEASURES BE ESTABLISHED?

STEP ONE

Where appropriate, department teams will have access to a copy of the company's Strategic Management Plan insofar as it relates to their particular part of the business. This provides the context and legitimises the development of individual action plans.

STEP TWO

(a) Individuals will construct their own six to eight outputs (i.e. what they personally contract to

---

6 Thanks are acknowledged to Dr Eddie Molloy for introducing the author to this concept which he labels Team Based Action Planning.

deliver) for the coming 12 months. They will also develop the specific Performance Measures (the standards of achievement/dates etc.) for each output.

(b) Individuals will list the topics/issues which they expect other members of their work team to address in the coming 12 months ("what I would like you to do for me").

STEP THREE

A meeting will be held where each member of the team (the team manager and the individual players) "show" their outputs for the coming 12 months.

Each individual will also receive the suggested outputs from their manager/peers. Other than simple clarification, the individual will simply accept the suggested outputs from their manager and peers. There will be no debate at this point.

STEP FOUR

After the meeting each individual reconstructs their listing of outputs, based on their original listings and the suggestions they have received from their peers/manager. Trade-off made between "what is needed" and "what is do-able".

STEP FIVE

A second meeting will be held whereby each member of the team (the team manager and the individual players) "show" their revised outputs/performance measures for the coming 12 months. If there are suggestions which individuals have decided not to progress, they will explain the rationale for this. The team can openly debate the quality of the individual performance plans at this point.

Once agreed, the performance plan becomes a contract between the individual manager and their boss/peers. While the overall process may seem slow (it is slow at the front-end of action plan design and agreement) it can be a highly effective way to implement strategic plans.

CHAPTER

PERFORMANCE
COACHING

PERFORMANCE COACHING SYSTEM: OVERVIEW

The objective of Performance Coaching is to improve current performance and to highlight developmental needs within the company. It involves:

• Generating data on existing performance levels

• Letting employees know what is expected of them through discussion of performance to date vs. the agreed performance measures

• Solving job-related problems which are blocking performance

• Providing feedback to increase motivation

• Coaching to improve performance and increase outputs

• Identifying training needs.

Performance Coaching therefore has four central components:

1 Observing and documenting performance

2 Conducting individual interim reviews

3 Identifying training and development needs

4 Coaching and supporting individual employees.

1
OBSERVE AND DOCUMENT PERFORMANCE

Each manager needs to have an accurate "fix" on the performance standards in the preceding period. This information can come from a variety of sources:

• Personal observation of behaviour

• Specific "outputs" achieved and/or not achieved

• Feedback from the employees' "customers" (internal or external).

Care should be taken that the performance data reflects the entire period under review and does not over-emphasise recent behaviours/outcomes while downplaying slightly more distant events.

2
CONDUCT INDIVIDUAL INTERIM REVIEWS

While practices differ from company to company, between one and two interim reviews are normally held each year.[1] Here the individual and the manager meet on a one-to-one basis to discuss performance progress since the last formal performance review. The outcome of this meeting is recorded on the Performance Management Form[2] and this influences the rating of the person at the end of year review.[3]

---

1 In well-managed organisations, feedback is given to employees on a continuous basis. The interim reviews refer to the process where the manager and employee specifically set time aside to formally review the progress made since the last formal performance review.

2 The format for this differs between companies. It is suggested that the interim review be built into the actual format to send a signal of importance about this event – otherwise it can be overlooked by managers pleading the "too-busy" syndrome.

3 In some companies, pay and performance are directly linked.

3
IDENTIFY TRAINING AND DEVELOPMENT NEEDS

As part of the interim review meetings, the training and development needs of individuals should be addressed. A specific section on the Performance Management Form should be designed to help managers work through this issue.[4]

4
COACHING AND SUPPORTING

Coaching is a proactive, action-based process. It provides an ongoing source of help to ensure that the employee succeeds by:

• Removing obstacles to progress

• Providing ongoing reinforcement of effective behaviour

• Giving authentic and timely feedback on missed targets or negative behaviour

• Implementing agreed training plans.

The goal of coaching is skill transference — ensuring people become sufficiently independent to do the job themselves.[5]

---

4 Some companies complete this at the beginning or the end of the performance review period. Mid-year is the optimum time in the cycle as it allows more time for the review to be completed satisfactorily (and not as an afterthought to the goal setting or the pay review.

5 A feedback skills questionnaire is included in Appendix E which will enable you to test your skills in the area of performance coaching.

PERFORMANCE COACHING MEETINGS

▶ **KEY STEPS**

- Put the employee at ease. State that the purpose of the session is to talk about how they are getting along vs. the objectives set at the start of the performance planning period and to see if there is anything you can do to help.

- Provide recognition for good performance, mentioning the specific measurement achievements and criteria.

Only a mediocre person is always at his best

Somerset Maughan

- Cover those areas where performance is satisfactory and explore the reasons why this is the case.

- Outline the areas where improvement is necessary and the effect that poor performance has on goal achievement.

- Ask for their views of the current work situation, suggestions for changes to overcome any roadblocks, etc.

- Agree a plan of action to overcome the issues raised in the discussion.

- End by expressing confidence that good performance will be maintained and, if appropriate, that problem areas will be corrected.

- Set a specific follow-up time to review the agreed plan of action (if necessary).

GIVING POSITIVE FEEDBACK

 OBJECTIVE

Use all available opportunities to encourage good performance by giving positive feedback.

 THE FOUR STEPS APPROACH

Alas the fearful unbelief is unbelief in yourself

Thomas Carlyle

1 Praise the employee immediately after the positive incident has occurred.

2 Tell the employee what they did right. Be specific.

3 Tell the employee how you feel about what they did and how it benefits the organisation.

4 Encourage them to do more of the same.

HOW TO RECOGNISE
ABOVE AVERAGE PERFORMANCE

▶ OBJECTIVE

Encourage continued performance of this kind. The recognition should be given as soon as possible after the above-average performance has occurred. The recognition should be given at a private meeting, which takes place in a formal setting.

▶ THE FOUR STEPS APPROACH

1 State specifically what the employee did that deserves recognition.

2 Express your personal satisfaction with this performance and, if appropriate, favourable comments by others.

3 Explain the impact of this performance — how it contributes to the success of the organisation and how it reflects upon the employee's skills and abilities.

4 Again, express your appreciation for this performance.

HOW TO RECOGNISE
CONSISTENT PROGRESS

▶ OBJECTIVE

To encourage the employees to maintain good performance. The recognition should be given as part of a casual or informal discussion.

▶ THE FOUR STEPS APPROACH

1 State specifically what the employee is doing that deserves recognition.

2 Express your satisfaction for the progress the employee is making.

3 Explain how this kind of performance contributes to the development of the employee and the success of the unit.

4 Again, express your appreciation for this performance.

HOW TO CORRECT
SUBSTANDARD PERFORMANCE

▶ **OBJECTIVE**

To agree upon actions to correct or prevent the problem in the future; not to make the employee admit fault or apologise for the problem. Hold the meeting when the problem occurs and when the employee can act on it. You may also need to address the particular issues at the quarterly review meeting.

▶ **THE FOUR STEPS APPROACH**

1 Put the employee at ease.

2 Specifically define the problem and the effect it has on accomplishing the goals of the assignment (focus on the problem behaviour, not the personality).

3 Ask for the employee's help and discuss their ideas to correct and/or prevent this problem.

4 Agree on actions to be taken by each of you. Ensure that the employee understands what is expected of them and set a specific follow-up time to review results of these actions.

5.7 THE PYGMALION EFFECT: CONFIDENT LEADERS PRODUCE CONFIDENT FOLLOWERS

Every excellent company we studied is clear on what it stands for, and takes the process of value shaping seriously. In fact, we wonder whether it is possible to be an excellent company without clarity on values and without having the right sort of values

Peters and Waterman, *In Search of Excellence*

Leaders who expect their followers to succeed exert a positive influence and obtain extraordinary short-term and long-term results. Their followers feel competent and enthusiastic and face tasks with the expectation of success. In contrast, managers who have doubts about people's ability will expect less of their employees and will treat them in a manner that reveals this lack of confidence — and it becomes a self-fulfilling prophesy ("you expect less and you get less").

Self-esteem is a crucial factor in the follower's ability to be successful. The development of individual potential is derived from the freeing power of self-esteem. If you regard yourself highly, you will expect more of yourself. The result: more aggressive goals and more impressive achievements. You need to show confidence in the people who work for you.

LEADING IN PERFORMANCE

Leaders who are successful at performance coaching have certain characteristics in common:

- A belief in their ability to develop the potential of their followers, to provide the appropriate amounts of direction and support that the followers need in order to be successful.

- An ability to establish and communicate goals that are challenging, yet realistic and attainable. Goals that are neither too easy nor too difficult are optimally motivating.

- Positive assumptions about the potential of others — an ability to see them as winners.

- A commitment to excellence and a genuine enthusiasm for what they do. Positive involvement, commitment, and intensity are contagious.

- A focus on the human aspects of the task in addition to a focus on procedures, conceptual frameworks and technology. Progress comes through people — great leaders have a superb ability to maximise the human talent and potential given to them.

- Most successful companies have a group of managers who can lead their employees to excellent performance levels. Excellent performance is a win-win; good for the company and good for the individual employee.

Managers are people who do things right, and leaders are people who do the right thing

Warren G. Bennis & Burt Nanus

ESTABLISHING
A PARTNERSHIP RELATIONSHIP

*The hammers
must be swung
in cadence,
when more
than one is
hammering the
iron*

Giordano Bruno

Managing performance is a joint management/employee effort. Central to this is the ability to develop a partnership relationship between a manager and employees. Conceptualising their role as a "partner" helps managers encourage commitment to agreed objectives and gives them a "coaching" rather than a "judging" role. It also gives them the responsibility to ensure that each of their people is performing "up to par".

When people know what to expect of each other and know what is expected of them, they are more likely to achieve work goals. Clarity around expectations is a necessary element of an effective partnership. The alternative is confusion about goals or roles and the interpersonal difficulties which often accompany this.

What is Partnership?
Having a share in an act or enterprise, playing on the same team or side

Penguin Concise Dictionary

 PERFORMANCE PARTNERSHIP

A central element in the Performance Management System is the establishment of a "partnership relationship" between managers and employees.

MOVING FROM "JUDGE" TO "COACH": THE MANAGEMENT PARTNERSHIP

A partnership relationship is a movement away from the traditional notion of a manager as "judge" towards the concept of the manager as "coach" with knock-on consequences for the type of behaviour exhibited.

Judge	Coach
Evaluative	Descriptive
Controlling	Problem-oriented
Detached	Empathetic
Superior	On the same team
Rigid	Flexible

Partnerships are most effective when the partners know what to expect of each other and know how to articulate these expectations candidly, but with concern for the other's self-esteem. Candour and concern for the other's self-esteem are, therefore, two key criteria for any partnership to work effectively.

The skills of "coaching" really come into play when managers are tasked with giving performance feedback.

GIVING FEEDBACK AT THE BI-ANNUAL PERFORMANCE COACHING MEETING

Positive anything is better than negative nothing

Elbert Hubbard

Performance Coaching is based on the assumption that people cannot learn and develop unless they receive feedback on how they are progressing. As people are an expensive resource, it makes sense to maximise their output by ensuring that everyone performs at their full potential. The rationale for giving performance feedback is that it will help sustain or improve performance. However, some skill is required when giving feedback, since if not done correctly it can result in the employees becoming offended, confused or even demotivated. There are some general rules about providing feedback which are detailed below.

Achieving good performance is a journey, not a destination

Kenneth H. Blanchard & Robert Lorber

The Performance Coaching Meeting is held once or twice each year depending on the particular company preference.

There are three central objectives for the meeting:

- To establish how well the employee is performing in relation to their objectives

- To provide coaching to ensure that future performance remains on track or is enhanced

- To plan training and development needs.

1
ACHIEVING UNDERSTANDING

The feedback given at the meeting should be specific rather than general. The person who is receiving feedback should be cited specific examples of the behaviour in question. It will then be much easier to understand what has been said rather than if the message is given only in terms of generalisations.

Specificity: For example, if a person is told that they do not listen, this is likely to be less helpful than if a particular instance can be cited where this behaviour was exhibited. If you can recall vividly a particular instance in which they missed a critical discussion point because of poor listening, then the person is more likely to be able to grasp the meaning of what is being said.

Key Point: Don't generalise about what kind of a "person" the individual is — give clear examples of behaviour.

KEEP THE LANGUAGE "SPECIFIC"

Examples of Specific and Non-Specific Language

A She doesn't communicate

vs.

B She does not explain changes in regulations to her people, resulting in their inability to keep up to date with procedures.

A He is a poor analyst

vs.

B He does not fully explore alternative courses of action before making decisions. This affects the potential benefit of decisions made.

A He is not demanding with his people

vs.

B He accepts his peers' and employees' opinions and recommendations without questioning them and without offering superior alternatives which he knows to exist.

GIVE RECENT EXAMPLES OF BEHAVIOUR

Timeliness: Other things being equal, recent examples of behaviour are better than old ones. In order for an individual to understand what has happened in a particular situation, they have to be able to recall the instance. What took place yesterday will be easier to recall than what took place last week or last year.

2
GAINING ACCEPTANCE

Parliament can compel people to obey or to submit, but it cannot compel them to agree

Winston Churchill

To get acceptance for feedback, it is important to establish at least a minimum foundation of trust. If John is to accept critical feedback from Ciara, then he needs to believe that Ciara's intention in giving the feedback is to be constructive.

Trust is built over time through candour — by being authentic — and by making every effort possible to maintain the other person's self-esteem.

COACH/MENTOR VS JUDGE

If a manager's tone of voice, facial expression, choice of words, and everything else communicates the impression, "I value you, and I really would like to help you, which is the reason why I am telling you this" then the employee will be more receptive to the message being communicated. If the manager merely rattles off a list of observations about the employee's behaviour in a non-constructive way, the impact of the feedback may be a worsening performance level.

DON'T JUDGE — DESCRIBE

In giving negative feedback to another person, the receiver will be more likely to accept it if the message is descriptive rather than evaluative. The sender should describe what happened and communicate the effect it had, as opposed to evaluating its goodness or badness, rightness or wrongness, in more general terms.

Before giving a person negative feedback of any kind, the sender should consider whether now is a good time to do so — whether the other person appears to be in a condition of readiness to receive information of this kind. If they appear, for example, to be angry, upset, or defensive, the answer is probably no. We can use the analogy of a radio transmitter (the manager). Signals sent will only be effective if the receiver (the employee) is switched on. As a manager, it is a key element of your role to create the necessary conditions in which feedback will be positively accepted.

3
ASSESSING ABILITY TO UTILISE FEEDBACK

Evaluation

is a time for

accounting; for

comparing

actions with

consequences;

for detecting

flaws and mak-

ing improve-

ments for plant-

ing the seeds of

future challenge

**Don Koberg and Jim
Bagnall**

The final criterion in providing "useful" feedback is that the recipient must be able to do something with it. Consider the following:

Suppose you feel that a particular person does not present ideas as forcefully and persuasively as he ought to, and you decide you want to tell him about this. This is still a pretty general feeling. Before saying anything, you should consider specifically what it is that prompts your feelings. You may think, for example, that he doesn't present his thoughts as well under some circumstances as you know he is capable of. Given in a positive, specific way, this may be quite useful feedback.

On the other hand, suppose you feel that the only thing that interferes with his ability to persuade, to carry his ideas over to a group forcibly, is that his accent is irritating. There may be little point in calling attention to this kind of issue (if you are really trying to be helpful).

Feedback can lead to improvements only when it is about things which can be changed!

DON'T OVERLOAD THE RECEIVER

Comparisons

are odious

• **Robert Burton**

When learning how to give feedback, we sometimes tend to overdo it. It's as though we were telling the receiver: "I have a list of reactions here. If you'll settle back for a few hours, I'll read them to you". Give feedback gently — a small chunk at a time as a follow-on to observed behaviour which you believe is non-productive.

Resist the tendency to overload the receiver. At all times try to answer positively the question "am I being helpful to this person?" Maintaining each person's self-esteem is a central part of an effective Performance Management System.

5.10

PROVIDING
NEGATIVE CORRECTIVE FEEDBACK

Don't make excuses – make good

Elbert Hubbard

One of the most difficult and most important responsibilities you face as a manager is dealing fairly and effectively with an employee whose performance is unsatisfactory.

For many managers, it is not easy to sit face-to-face with an employee and discuss performance shortcomings. Some managers who wish to avoid confrontations simply ignore poor performance in the hope that it will self-correct. Others may consider non-confrontational ways to deal with the issue, e.g. internal transfers or making a half-hearted effort to counsel the person, hoping that performance will improve over time.

Don't let the performance appraisal be a one–sided lecture. Give your staff a chance to talk

Margie Markham

None of these courses of action are acceptable. They risk your reputation for excellence, damage the morale of other employees and ultimately are also unfair to the individual involved.

If you see a person struggling with the requirements of the job, don't wait until appraisal time to sit down and talk about it. Delay only aggravates the problem for everyone. Identify the deficiency, conduct a performance counselling session and work out a specific plan to improve performance.

Key Point: Partnership relationships are built on a foundation of people being authentic. Avoiding a performance problem is not authentic behaviour.

REMOVING OBSTACLES TO PERFORMANCE

Regular performance coaching ensures that employees remain on course towards attaining their agreed objectives. Since employees do not perform their required tasks in isolation, a range of factors may affect their ability to achieve results. Generally it is within the control of management to alter or remove obstacles which prevent employees from performing effectively. Goals may need to be modified during the course of a review period, e.g. as a result of a change in external markets. If goals are not reviewed during this interim period, then proper performance appraisal at the end of the year may not be possible.

Understanding should precede judging

Louis Brandeis

In some cases, however, goals are not achieved as a result of circumstances within people's control. These situations may be overcome by:

• Coaching

• Training

• Performance Counselling.

When objectives are not being met, it is the responsibility of the manager to confront the underperformance issue. Understanding the reasons for underperformance is a necessary first step to finding an appropriate solution.

IDENTIFYING TRAINING NEEDS

▶ **SELF-ASSESSMENT OF TRAINING NEEDS**

One of the key goals of the Performance Coaching meeting is to collect data on training needs. The way to do this is to ask employees to list the key skills or areas in which they need to improve. These areas should be related to the current job which they are performing. You should try to get "evidence" for the stated needs (e.g. problems in the current job, changing future job requirements, etc.) to support their assessment.

Although it can be useful to prepare a list of topics as a way to "prompt" this, one inherent danger in this approach is that it can become a "training menu" with items selected on the basis of "attractiveness" rather than being an identified training need which will add value to the business.

A useful model to follow is outlined below.

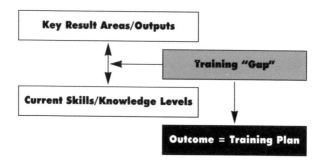

PERSONAL DEVELOPMENT — EXAMPLE

(The following questions are usually helpful in establishing training needs):

A What specific steps were taken in the past year to improve overall performance (acquisition of experience, knowledge and/or skills)?

- Sales training programme (six days) completed in August.
- Read three books on the topic of sales (Effective Sales Closing, Territory Management and Overcoming Objections).

B How has this affected performance?

- 110 per cent of sales target at this point.
- Much more confidence in dealing with clients' objections.
- More rational territory management.

C What development actions are planned for the coming year?

- Complete "area management" sales course (two days in August).
- Listen to "The Complete Sales Course" (20 audio tapes) in car while working.
- Continue to refine sales closure technique through discussions with the other sales reps.

CHAPTER

6

PERFORMANCE
REVIEW

6.1 WHY HAVE A PERFORMANCE REVIEW?

The purpose of the annual performance review is to discuss the appraisee's progress towards meeting the goals which were set for the preceding year. A well-conducted Performance Review provides several organisational benefits. Specifically:

Acknowledges Positive Performance

It provides a vehicle through which positive performance can be formally acknowledged and, therefore, an opportunity for motivating the appraisee to continue to perform at this level.

Corrects Poor Performance

It provides a formal means through which poor performance can be documented and corrective action taken.

Equitable Basis of Salary Adjustments

It provides a mechanism on which to base salary change decisions.

Management Learning Tool

It acts as a management learning tool. By obtaining feedback from the appraisee, a company can learn about actions taken (what worked well and what didn't) in terms of facilitating better employee performance.

PERFORMANCE REVIEW ROADMAP

A roadmap to guide the appraiser through the stages involved in carrrying out a performance review, is set out below. While individual companies emphasise different elements of the performance review process, the roadmap presented sets out the key stages which are followed by many successful companies.

STEP 1
APPRAISEE IS INFORMED AND CARRIES OUT A SELF-APPRAISAL

It is useless for the sheep to pass resolutions in favour of vegetarianism, while the wolf remains of a different opinion

William Ralph Inge

The manager gives the appraisee advance notice (usually one week) of the day/time when the performance review meeting is to take place.

In many companies, it is standard practice for the appraisee to complete a self-appraisal form and return it to the manager a few days prior to the meeting. The information gleaned from the self-appraisal form will assist the manager in completing the draft appraisal and in planning the review meeting strategy.

WHY DO EMPLOYEES COMPLETE A SELF-APPRAISAL?

The criticism which is most often levelled against appraisal systems is that they are "top down" — employees feel that it is a pre-ordained process over which they have little control. For best results, people need to feel that they are involved in the process rather than see it as something that is "done to them." The self-appraisal mechanism goes a long way towards meeting this need.

STEP 2
MANAGER COLLECTS INFORMATION

Preparation on the part of the manager (or the lack of it) sends a clear signal to the appraisee of the importance which the organisation attaches to performance appraisal. The meeting will be more productive if the manager has done the groundwork before hand.

The manager prepares for the performance review by collecting relevant information. Specifically:

1 By talking to people who have worked with the appraisee and getting an input from the appraisee's customers — both internal and external.

2 By reviewing any available written records, e.g. the previous appraisal, job analysis forms, the appraisee's self-appraisal, performance results to date etc.

When an appraisal system is operating effectively, no new/surprising information will emerge at the review meeting; any information that has not been picked up through the coaching sessions should come to light by the manager doing "homework" prior to the review.

STEP 3
MANAGER COMPLETES INTERIM APPRAISAL

Using the standard form, the manager prepares an assessment of how the appraisee has done on the basis of the information collected and personal observation of performance.

The manager's appraisal at this stage is written as a draft as it may change depending on input received from the appraisee at the Performance Review Meeting. It is good practice to complete the appraisal form in full, including the rating section. The copy provided to the reviewee should have the word "draft" written on the cover sheet to signify clearly that it is not a "fait accompli".

The manager gives a copy of the assessment of the appraisee's performance to the appraisee in advance of the formal review.

JUDGE RESULTS NOT EFFORT

- Ensuring that the measurement of performance levels is as objective as possible is crucial for the effectivenss of a performance management system. The key focus in the appraisal is therefore on the outputs achieved — the extent to which the reviewee achieved or did not achieve their goals. Excellent performance is not about levels of effort. The emphasis is on the outputs/results/tangible achievements that add value to the business.

- The manager needs to know the specific goals that the appraisee is to be measured against. It is then the responsibility of the manager to make a decision on how well the appraisee has performed in the light of those goals. By making this decision in advance of the review meeting, the manager thereby avoids the risk of being influenced by the persuasive ability of an appraisee.

STEP 4
CONDUCTING THE PERFORMANCE REVIEW MEETING

The performance review should take place in a suitable environment. The meeting should not be disturbed by people coming in or out of the office or by the appraiser taking incoming phone calls.

In conducting the Performance Review Meeting, the appraiser should:

1 Explain the purpose of the meeting and the ground rules

2 Reinforce positive outcomes

3 Negatively reinforce poor results

4 Give a managerial appraisal rating

5 Decide on salary/bonus adjustment

6 Conclude the meeting appropriately.

Each of the above points will be covered in more detail in the following pages.

1. EXPLAIN THE PURPOSE OF THE MEETING AND THE GROUND RULES

The manager explains the purpose of the meeting and the ground rules. The following is an example of the type of opening statement a manager would make:

"Good morning, Tom. I am looking forward to this meeting — it gives us an opportunity to look at the performance results for last year. Here's how I suggest the meeting will run.

Firstly, we will discuss your performance results, comparing them with the goals we set at the beginning of the year.

Secondly, we will agree a final rating for the year which will be based on the company's 4-scale rating categories.[1]

Thirdly, I will inform you of your salary increase.

Throughout the meeting, you will have an opportunity to participate in the discussion. This is a two-way meeting, Tom. It will not work unless you are actively involved. Do you have any questions at this point?"

2. REINFORCE POSITIVE OUTCOMES

- Performance review meetings should commence with a focus on the "positives", as a key concern is to maintain the self-esteem of the appraisee.

- The manager should recognise both satisfactory and above-average performance.

- Particular attention should be paid to any areas which have improved since the last review. Specific examples should be used and any measurement criteria available should be referred to.

- Try to get behind the reasons for good performance. If, for example, it is due to increased effort on the part of the appraisee, this may send a signal that the reward structure is working well. If improved performance can be attributed to an expanded skill base, this provides important information for the company's trainers.

---

1 This differs from company to company.

- The manager should seek information on any additional assistance that the company could provide which would accelerate any increase in performance effectiveness.

3. NEGATIVELY REINFORCE POOR RESULTS

- The manager should try and elicit the underlying reasons for poor performance. The effect that under-performance has upon goal achievement should be explained and the reason why improvement is necessary.

- At all times, the emphasis should be placed on the performance, not the personality. This keeps the focus on what can be changed. It also helps maintain the appraisee's self-esteem. In the event of an emotional response on the part of the appraisee, discussion should be centred around the achievements.

- The "no surprises" rule stands; any problem areas should have come to the surface through quarterly reviews, coaching sessions etc. If a major surprise does emerge (e.g. the printing machine which was to be installed on January 10 did not arrive until October 31 which explains why only 5,000 cards were printed) the manager has one of two options. They can either discuss the issue and make a decision on the spot or postpone the meeting to check the details. The first option is appropriate when the issue involved is of no major consequence.

- The appraisee's assistance should be requested in resolving the performance problem. The objective is to obtain employee commitment to specific action plans, identifying no more than two to three high-priority areas.

The future is made in the present

Kelly Andrews

4. MANAGERIAL APPRAISAL RATING

The manager should explain the reasons for the rating given to the appraisee on the draft appraisal form. This is often a difficult area. Depending on the particular organisation, some ratings can be seen as "mediocre" (e.g. in one large financial services institution, a rating of less than "3" on a 1–4 scale was simply unacceptable to most people regardless of the level of performance). The final rating will not be decided until the formal Performance Review.

Should a salary review be given at the same meeting?

There are two schools of thought with regard to discussing performance ratings and salary at the same meeting. One view suggests that the discussion on rating and salary should be an integral part of the formal review. If the company's philosophy is to link pay with performance, this link should be made explicit — how better to do this than to tie both together at the same time/same place. An alternative argument is that the discussion on salary increase should take place some time after the performance review meeting in order not to detract from the importance of the central issue — how performance matches up against goals set at the start of the planning period.

How do we achieve consistency across management groups *vis-à-vis* ratings of subordinates?

In order to ensure consistency of ratings across groups, a system can be put in place to "test" the ratings that a manager gives to their appraisees. This is reviewed by other managers who have people reporting to them. The manager's peers usually have a good intuitive understanding of when a manager is working "too hard" or "too soft". This is a useful levelling mechanism and can also be used where a new system is being introduced. As people gain more proficiency in carrying out a performance review, the need for such a system can be reviewed/relaxed.

5 SALARY/BONUS ADJUSTMENT

- In conducting the discussion on salary change the employee should be told about the amount of the increase (both per cent and actual figure) and the date on which it is to take effect.

- The basis of the calculation of any salary increase needs to be explained. Where there is a specific pay-for-performance philosophy, the appraisee should be able to see the relationship between an improvement in performance and a salary increase (or decrease).

6 CONCLUDING THE PERFORMANCE REVIEW MEETING

- At the end of the meeting, the manager should re-cap on the issues that have been raised and there should be a written account of items agreed.

- Where an appraisee is surprised at or disagrees with the manager's assessment this can be recorded on the appraisal form.[2]

---

2 Every effort is usually made to resolve this type of issue locally. If manager and appraisee continue to fail to reach agreement, the company's appeals mechanism may need to be invoked.

- At the conclusion of the appraisal discussion both the manager and appraisee sign the performance appraisal form.

- The manager then thanks the appraisee and ends the discussion on an encouraging note.

 CONCLUSION

If (phew!) you have made it this far, compliment yourself on having acquired a managerial skill.

6.3 COMMON APPRAISAL PITFALLS

On the preceding pages, we sketched the performance review roadmap and the key milestones along the way. Some of the more common errors that appraisers make in dealing with appraisees are outlined below:

1
▶ FAILURE TO SPECIFY CLEARLY PROBLEM OR BEHAVIOUR CAUSING CONCERN

In trying to reinforce or change an appraisee's behaviour, the specific behaviour must be identified. An appraiser might say "your performance has not been up to scratch". This statement is too general. The appraiser needs to be specific. A statement such as "your scrap rate is 15 per cent over standard" or "you have been late three days in the last month" leaves the appraisee in no doubt as to how they are under-performing.

When giving recognition, the good performance should also be specifically identified so that the appraisee knows exactly the type of behaviour that is valued and should be continued.

2
▶ TENDENCY TO DISCUSS PROBLEMS IN TERMS OF PERSONALITY OR PERSONALITY CHARACTERISTICS

Another common fault is the tendency to discuss problems in terms of personality or personality characteristics. Instead of saying, "you have been absent ten times and have failed to meet production schedules" some appraisers express the problem as "you are lazy" or "you have no interest in working". The appraiser should stick to what they can observe. Do not label people: it often provokes strong negative/defensive reactions — which do not lead to the problem being resolved.

3
TENDENCY TO DEAL WITH MORE THAN ONE TOPIC IN A CONVERSATION

Employees can understand, respond to, and act upon only one or two issues at a time. The appraiser must identify the crucial performance issue and focus the mind of the appraisee on it. Don't allow yourself to be side-tracked by unrelated issues or try to deal with more than one concern at a time. Keep it simple. Deal with other topics by setting another time to discuss them.

4
TENDENCY ONLY TO IDENTIFY A PROBLEM, NOT DEVELOP AN ACTION PLAN

It is not uncommon for the appraiser and appraisee to agree that a problem exists while at the same time failing to develop any plan of action to overcome it. A problem is more likely to be solved if an action plan is developed. Just as it is important to identify specifically the problems, the action plans must also be specific. Just saying "do better" or "try harder" may not lead to positive results, if for no other reason than the employee does not know specifically what to do.

5
FAILURE TO SET A SPECIFIC FOLLOW-UP TIME

Often appraisers may discuss a significant problem with an employee, and both agree to do something about it, but the appraiser never follows up to see if the actions were carried out. Some appraisees listen politely, but realise the appraiser will not follow up on action items and consequently do nothing about them. The appraiser should set specific follow-up times and abide by them. In the words of Stephen Sondheim, "Having just a vision is no solution; everything depends on execution."

CHAPTER

7

PROJECT
TEAMS

7.1

INTRODUCTION

A team is a small number of people with complementary skills who are committed to a common purpose, performance goals, and approach for which they hold themselves mutually accountable

Jon R. Katzenbach and Douglas K. Smith,
The Wisdom of Teams

Most managers will be familiar with the arguments put forward to support the benefits of working in teams. Indeed it is difficult to find a current management magazine which does not make reference to the "wisdom" of teamworking. From the early concept of Quality Circles (circa 1970) to more recent experimentation with full self-direction, teamworking can positively affect morale, drive innovation and increase productivity. Overall the evidence to support the benefits of teamworking is impressive.[1] This raises the puzzling question, "why do so few organisations utilise teams?"

 WHY DO SO FEW ORGANISATIONS UTILISE TEAMS?

Despite the potential benefits noted above, few organisations utilise teams. The reason for this is that effective teamworking requires a complex social organisa-

---

1 See, for example, the work completed by Waterman (1994), *The Frontiers of Excellence* and Katzenbach and Smith (1993), *The Wisdom of Teams.*

tion which is difficult to launch and even more difficult to maintain. Full team-based organisations are complex social systems. To survive they require significant organisational support including team systems design, rewards which reinforce teamwork, an effective meeting/communications structure, and a supportive company culture. While most references to teamworking mention the upsides, few dwell on the downsides — the significant level of organisational energy which needs to be invested to make teamworking effective.

BRIDGING THE GAP: THE ESTABLISHMENT OF TURBO-CHARGED PROJECT TEAMS

The development of what we have labelled "Turbo-charged" Project Teams[2] offers a mechanism through which an organisation can get the benefits of teamworking while avoiding many of the downsides and organisational constraints listed. It is the organisational equivalent of ice cream without the calories.

Project teams differ from work teams in that they are set up to tackle a specific problem or difficulty. The team remains in existence for as long as the problem remains; once the particular problem has been solved, the team is disbanded. By their nature, project teams are clearly focused and by working through the process set out in this chapter, they can become "turbo-charged". This structure offers three specific benefits to the organisation:

---

2 The term turbo-charged first emerged in conversation with Tom McGurk, Plant Manager of Wyeth Medica in Ireland. As a "Deming disciple", Tom is heavily focused on "quality", defined as excellence in design aligned with excellence in execution.

1 **Bolted On** Given that project teams are "bolted on" to the existing organisation architecture, they do not need a cultural shift to support them.

2 **Fast Performance** Turbo-charged project teams, carefully constructed, begin to perform extremely quickly. Individuals who come together to form any team bring particular strengths, weaknesses, and specialist skills. They often come from a variety of backgrounds and hold different positions of power within the organisation. Given this diversity, it takes time for them to become accustomed to working together as a group.

3 **Safe Experiment** The short shelf-life of project teams provides a safe mechanism for organisations to experiment/pilot the concept of team-based working.

 TELESCOPING THE FIVE-STAGE LIFE CYCLE

In order to understand the turbo-charged team concept, we have to explore the normal five-stage process of team formation and operation. Academic research and experience in working with teams highlights that all newly formed teams go through a five-stage life cycle (often labelled Forming, Storming, Norming, Performing and Mourning). The benefit of turbo-charging the start-up of a project team (by working through a clearly defined process) is that the team moves to the performance stage very quickly — the organisational equivalent of being guided by a route map rather than stumbling through the woods.

You can turbo-charge the start-up of a project team by addressing the following six questions:

1 What is our purpose?

2 Which people should we select?

3 What is the role of each person?

4 What strategy will we use to achieve our purpose?

5 What are the key interfaces with people outside of our group?

6 How will we use feedback to monitor our performance?

For project teams (which have by definition a short shelf-life), speed is a key performance issue; they need to move quickly through the first three stages (Forming, Storming and Norming) of their life cycle to begin performance. By working through these seven questions, time spent in the first three stages can be greatly reduced, leaving the team with more time to spend in the performing stage (getting the job done).

An overview of the process is outlined in Figure 1. A detailed description on the individual elements follows in the text.

FIGURE 1
Establishing Work Teams

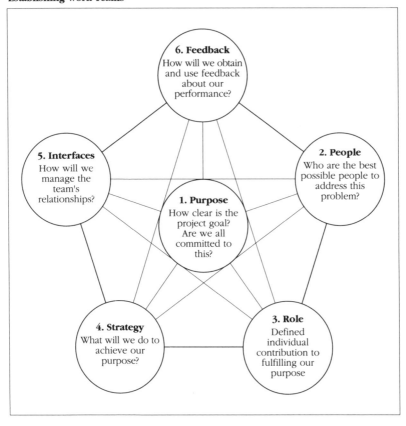

STEP ONE: CLEAR TEAM PURPOSE

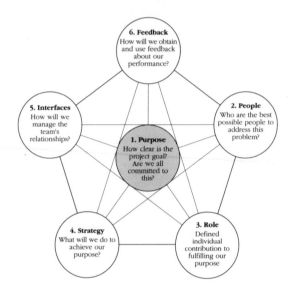

▶ PROJECT PURPOSE: SETTING "CRYSTAL CLEAR" GOALPOSTS

It is critically important that each team member is clear on the objectives for the specific project and is committed to them. Goals set should be realistic, measurable and agreed by the team members.[3] The first law of psychology is that people don't resist their own ideas; get everyone on the team involved in constructing the goalposts.

---

3 Realistically, in some cases, the project may have been "handed down" by senior management; however, many of the points still apply to ensure acceptance of project purpose.

▶ WRITING A PROJECT GOAL STATEMENT

A well-constructed project goal statement provides team purpose. It is the first step to be taken in the establishment of a turbo-charged team.[4] The written statement should contain the following information:

- The particular result to be attained ("what")

- A target date for completion ("when")

- The overall project cost ("how much").

---

4 The relatively small amount of time spent in constructing the project goal statement will be repaid by the time saved later.

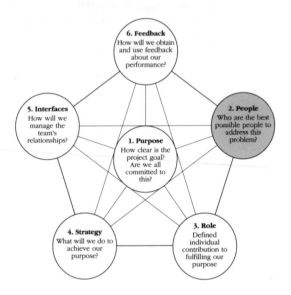

SELECTION OF PEOPLE FOR PROJECT TEAMS

This addresses the question, "Who are the best possible people to address the problem?" It is important that each member of the team is interested in the project and willing to participate. A key dilemma for most organisations is that the people "whom you can least afford to release", are the very people who ensure a project's success. Putting the best available people on the team is the surest way to influence the outcome.

Self-selection is an obvious place to start (volunteers are better than conscripts). However, if particular expertise or experience is required, participants may be "drafted" onto teams to ensure that the basic skills are in place to meet the project objectives.

PERSONNEL SELECTION CHECKLIST

It is important that the project team develops the right mix of skills. Essentially, team skill requirements fall into three categories:

- Technical or functional expertise

- Problem-solving and decision-making skills

- Communication and interpersonal skills.

For complex or particularly important projects, an identification of training needs may be conducted to establish training requirements for team members. These skills are then put in place prior to the commencement of the project. For simpler tasks, ideally each team member should possess the following characteristics:

- Be knowledgeable about the area

- Be enthusiastic about the team's task

- Possess the necessary skills to complete the required tasks.

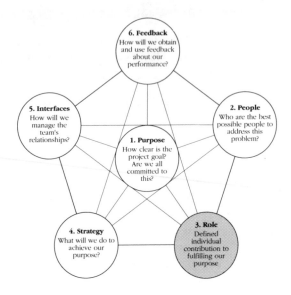

WHO'S WHO?

There are certain roles which need to be assigned to members of the project team to ensure the smooth functioning of the group. Each member of an orchestra needs to know their individual instrument and the overall piece of music; in similar vein, team members need to know the overall project purpose (see earlier points) and their place in the show. Establishing who is responsible for what and by when is a critically important part of the team initiation cycle. For small teams, two key project team roles usually need to be decided:

Team Leader/Facilitator   This person monitors the progress of the group's activities. In some project groups, this function can rotate.

Recorder   Usually someone takes minutes at each meeting and distributes these to the group post-meeting. This again can be a rotating position, so that everyone has involvement in the process.

MUTUAL RESPONSIBILITY

Although each project team has a team leader, this often tends to be less "hierarchical" than a management role which exists in the "normal" organisation structure. Within teams, each member of the group normally has an equal say, and has joint responsibility to achieve the group goals. In essence, the team must establish a social contract among its members that relates to their purpose and which guides how they will work together as the project unfolds.

SOCIAL ROLES: HELPING PEOPLE TO WORK EFFECTIVELY

The social roles of the group must also be decided on. The team needs to decide how it will work together to achieve its purpose (what are the groundrules?). These involve looking at such issues as: challenging, interpreting, supporting, integrating, and summarising. Although these processes do not exist straight away, they will evolve over time, and will do so more quickly if team members are aware that they are an integral part of working effectively in teams.

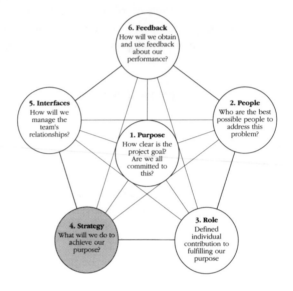

Once the purpose of the team has been established, and each member understands their role within the group, the next issue is to decide on the specific steps the team is going to take to achieve its goal — the strategy.

A useful way to progress this is to construct a series of action steps (what is required, who is responsible, the timeline involved etc.). This document (the "Project Plan") will not necessarily be definitive at this planning stage, but will change and be revised to ensure that work is progressing in the right direction.

The important questions to be answered under this heading include:

- How and when will resources be allocated?

- How will schedules be set?

- How will we check that schedules are being adhered to?

- How will the team make and modify its decisions?

- How often should the team meet, where and for how long?

In complex projects, team members will be engaged in diverse activities. Scheduling meetings and activities in advance can help to ensure full participation and co-ordination of the team activities. The logistics of the team's meetings and other activities should be decided at this early stage.

STEP FIVE: INTERFACES

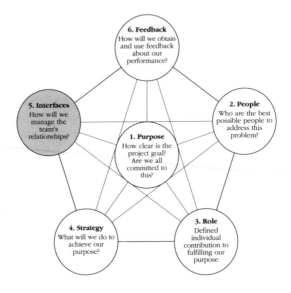

6. Feedback
How will we obtain and use feedback about our performance?

5. Interfaces
How will we manage the team's relationships?

2. People
Who are the best possible people to address this problem?

1. Purpose
How clear is the project goal? Are we all committed to this?

4. Strategy
What will we do to achieve our purpose?

3. Role
Defined individual contribution to fulfilling our purpose

► EXTERNAL INTERFACES

Teams do not work in isolation; they are stitched into other parts of the organisation. The degree of "fit" with other processes and departments of the organisation will, in part, determine the success of the project. In order to facilitate this, the project should be reviewed by asking the following questions:

- Whose approval is required?

- Whose commitment is critical to success?

- Who has relevant information?

- Who will be affected by the project?

▶ TEAM INTERFACES: HANDLING CONFLICT

Conflict can and will arise during group discussions. This can be very healthy, as it exposes the group to more than one point of view. It is important, however, that conflict is centred around the task and not about personal issues. The role of the team leader is to ensure that any conflict which arises is not damaging to the group.

STEP SIX: FEEDBACK

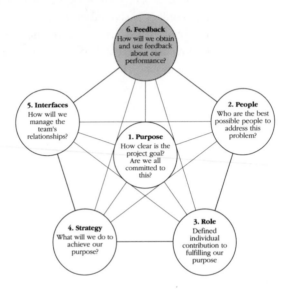

There is a bounty of research results which indicate that feedback is highly motivating. In relation to project teams, decisions need to be made as regards how feedback will be obtained and used both during the project and after the project has been completed.

Specifically, decisions need to be made as regards how to determine each of the following:

1 How is the project progressing? (review)

2 What actions are needed to resolve problems?

3 How should the outcome be presented, i.e. written report/formal presentation?

4 How well did we accomplish what we set out to do, and what did we learn?

5 What went well in the project?

6 What could have been done differently?

7 What actions need to be taken to ensure success in future projects?

For all of the reasons noted, project teams are an effective tool in the armoury of high-performance organisations. Try them: those companies which utilise this structure unleash a powerful force.

TRAINING
NEEDS

8.1 INTRODUCTION

In some companies Training Managers are well respected, command substantial resources (both budgetary and headcount) and exercise a high degree of "organisational influence". In others, they continuously have trouble in getting people to attend programmes ("we were busy, so Tom could not be released"), have low budgets ("it was a tough year — we cut our training budget by 58 per cent") and are concerned more with personal survival than developing organisational solutions or strategic capacity.

How can these two very different scenarios be explained? While a myriad of factors are potentially at play here, a key reason is that less successful Training Managers simply fail to convince companies of their worth to the business. Training is too often seen as a cost item, an activity of indulgence when times are good rather than a fundamental investment in business development to ensure future success. Many Training Managers, albeit inadvertently, help to reinforce this view by ignoring their most powerful weapon — a systematic identification of training needs upon which key business solutions can be developed.

The identification of training needs is a key tool in linking the role of the Training Manager with business performance and future growth. This chapter sets out a simple four-step procedure to collect and analyse data on training needs.

▶ TRAINING AS A "SOLUTION"

In most organisations training is essentially seen as a "solution", a method to bridge an identified "gap" in individual or organisational performance. A central point is that effective training starts with good diagnosis. Where managers put too much emphasis on training "delivery" and too little on the identification of organisational issues where training can provide support, training becomes a solution against which no corresponding "problem" has been identified.

Training is a system within a system, the larger system being the organisation itself. Training as a sub-system should positively affect organisational performance. If the training implemented does not support the achievement of organisational goals, a company undoubtedly has better uses for its resources.

UNDERLYING PHILOSOPHY AND TIMESCALE

An identification of training needs is concerned with examining current performance issues and anticipating future organisation changes. It addresses the central question: "Can training provide a solution for currently identified organisation problems or help us to exploit future opportunities?"

A training need exists when a "blockage" is in place that hinders current or future performance and which can be overcome by training. Training cannot always provide a solution or even the most economic solution (e.g. it may be cheaper or more effective to recruit better qualified personnel than to train existing people; it may be cheaper to alter the process or machinery, attempt to obviate the need for a job to be done etc.).

Key Point: The overall objective of identifying and addressing training needs is to enhance organisational performance.

One useful way to categorise the underlying philosophy of a training intervention is provided in Figure 1.

FIGURE 1
Identification of Training Needs: Key perspectives

Name	Remedial Training	Readiness Training	Speculative Development
Focus	Gaps in current operating performance	Anticipated gaps arising from future operating requirements which are clearly understood	Possible gaps that might arise in the future which are not yet fully understood
Timescale	Short-Term	Mid-Term	Long-Term

 IDENTIFICATION OF TRAINING NEEDS: ROAD MAP

There are essentially six steps to be followed in the systematic identification of training needs. These are outlined diagramatically in Figure 2 and subsequently developed in the following pages.

FIGURE 2
Methodology: Identification of Training Needs

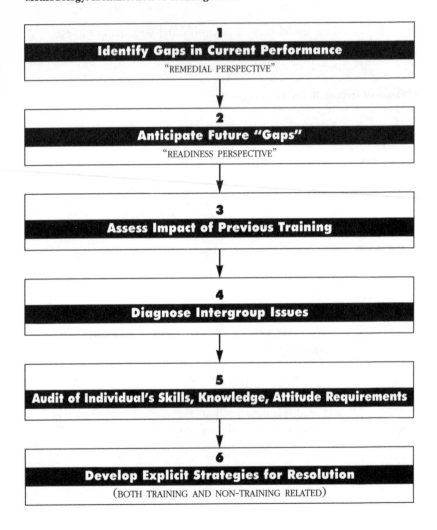

1	
Identify Gaps in Current Performance	
"REMEDIAL PERSPECTIVE"	

2
Anticipate Future "Gaps"
"READINESS PERSPECTIVE"

3
Assess Impact of Previous Training

4
Diagnose Intergroup Issues

5
Audit of Individual's Skills, Knowledge, Attitude Requirements

6
Develop Explicit Strategies for Resolution
(BOTH TRAINING AND NON-TRAINING RELATED)

STEP ONE: GAPS IN CURRENT PERFORMANCE — REMEDIAL TRAINING

A problem well stated is a problem half solved

Albert Einstein

A precursor to an effective identification of training needs is to understand the key business requirements. Information about current business problems/opportunities provides the foundation stone of effective training interventions. This information can be "uncovered" in a number of different ways. For example, reading published company reports can provide a useful insight into an organisation's mission, vision or key directions.

Measures or specific performance indicators are a second way to "access" current difficulties or likely areas where the Training Manager should focus attention. What symptoms are likely indicators of present faults in the organisation? Some examples are listed below.

- Performance appraisals highlight that ...

- Labour turnover is higher than the industry average

- People complain that communications are particularly poor

- Complaints from customers indicate ...

- Morale, as measured by climate surveys, is declining

- Standards of performance at the company or individual worker level are falling

- It takes a long time/high cost for employees to become fully effective

• High rates of waste materials/quality rejects.

These symptoms are often not independent. Several symptoms may provide evidence of one basic problem, e.g. customer complaints and high product wastage rate may indicate insufficient job training. Sometimes, one symptom may indicate several faults, e.g. labour turnover may indicate poor hiring and low morale.

A third data collection possibility under this heading is to get input from managers or a vertical slice of people within the organisation either through direct interviews, questionnaires or focus groups.

2

Will training help? Of the performance gaps identified, which of these could be positively influenced by training? Which are non-training related?

3

Are our competitors ahead of us, and in what areas? What external benchmark information do we have? External benchmarking (visits to competitor companies in the same industry or "best-in-class" companies) is a particularly useful way to assess the "height of the competitive hill" to be climbed.

Key Point: As in any case of problem-solving, you need to identify the problem carefully before you can effect a solution.

▶ MOVING FROM "REMEDIAL" TO "READINESS"

The preceding points are useful in understanding the current operation — they provide a "what exists" snapshot about current issues faced. However, an identification of training needs analysis based solely on a historical focus is incomplete. Training plans based on this tend to be remedially focused and somewhat short term. In contrast, an identification of training needs which focuses on "future" organisational requirements can be deemed as a "readiness" index, allowing the organisation to plan for/capitalise on business opportunities.

The central question addressed under this heading is whether a company's strategic plans include future business directions/strategies. If so, are these different from what currently exists and how will this affect training requirements in the organisation? Under this heading we should look for changes in:

1 Product or Service
    (a) Total demand
    (b) Nature of demand
    (c) Mix
    (d) New markets

2 Processes
    (e) Procedures
    (f) Methods

3 Personnel

(g) Replacements

(h) Supply

(i) Educational qualifications

4 Legislation

(j) What changes/impact?

5 Political Situation

(k) Nationally

(l) Locally

6 Company Goals

(m) Profitability, service standards etc.

7 Stated Values

(n) Innovation, teamwork etc.

MICROWORLDS: THE CREATION OF "FUTURE" SCENARIOS

One particularly interesting way to determine future development needs is the creation of "Microworlds". These are a range of realistic "what if" scenarios (essentially changes in the external business context) which would seriously impact the business (e.g. if the price of a barrel of oil rose to $60 what impact would this have on the revenues of the oil companies). Once the scenarios are created, senior management subsequently develop implementation plans to cope with these.

The most publicised example of this mechanism being used in practice is the Royal Dutch Shell Company. While the company surrounds its activities in great secrecy, they argue that this approach to the identification of management development needs significantly upgrades the quality of strategic management thinking and organisational "preparedness".

ASSEMBLING "MEANS": SPECULATIVE TRAINING AS A STRATEGIC GAMBLE

Another possible way to explore training needs is to invest in the development of strategic capability. This might involve training managers along a broad front about general economic conditions, the actions of competitors or providing new skills, e.g. problem diagnosis/solving. It might allow people to experiment with new technologies (within Hewlett-Packard people are encouraged to take products home and to experiment with them). As their capability levels develop, managers are encouraged to exploit relevant opportunities which they may have previously been unaware of (overcoming the "they don't know what they don't know" syndrome).

This notion of identifying training needs reverses conventional logic. Rather than developing plans and subsequently seeking to build internal human resource capabilities, some companies develop capabilities (knowledge and skills) and then encourage the development of business plans to exploit them. There are a couple of examples of this within Ireland.

EXAMPLE

In 1993 a large Irish multinational company decided to hire a number of graduate students and place them in "learning" positions throughout the organisation. While there was an obvious benefit for the graduates, this was not done for good "corporate citizenship" reasons.

The thinking was that the company would eventually benefit from an injection of new ideas.

A key point here is that the actual benefit cannot be calculated in advance. It follows that speculative training is a strategic gamble, i.e. a company decides to put the skills in place in order to respond to future strategic opportunities if and when they arise.

This concept can be captured diagramatically as follows:

Traditional Approach	Alternative Approach
Ends (Where do we want to get to?)	**Means** (Put the skills in practice)
Ways (How will we get there?)	**Ways** (Create new ways)
Means (Establish the means to do this)	**Ends** (Envision new ends)

STEP THREE: EVALUATING THE IMPACT OF PREVIOUS TRAINING

The effectiveness of previous training programmes can provide a "guideline" on what may work in the future. The simple question "What training has been conducted in the past?" can provide a useful way to predict the type of training intervention which will be most effective. This recognises the organisation-specific or cultural dimension to the implementation of new knowledge, skills, or attitudes.

▶ EXAMPLE

In one large multinational company in North County Dublin, the Managing Director asked a new Training Manager to run a series of "supervisory development programmes". The Managing Director explained that she was not happy with the supervisory group's commitment to the organisation and this should become a key part of the programme design.

On further research the Training Manager discovered that several similar programmes were run previously without any obvious impact on the problem. This suggested that another training programme might not solve the "supervisory problem" and that alternatives needed to be considered. The Training Manager approached the Managing Director with this insight and they eventually constructed an organisational development programme which addressed the real issues within the supervisory group which were blocking commitment.

STEP FOUR: DIAGNOSING INTERGROUP LEVEL ISSUES

An identification of training needs should also focus on issues at the intergroup level. In recent times there has been a growing recognition that inter-group/inter-functional effectiveness is a critical dimension of organisational performance. While historically most organisations are designed on a functional basis (marketing, finance, human resources etc.), most processes (the way work actually "flows" through an organisation) are cross-functional. Thus, work "between-the-boxes" has a profound impact on organisational performance and success.

Useful questions to address under this heading include:

- Are the goals of each section complimentary or competitive?

- Are the roles of each section crystal clear?

- Are there areas of either "underlap" or "overlap" in responsibility for particular tasks?

- Are there any areas where intra-function effectiveness is blocked? Why?

- Are there poor working relationships/scapegoating between shifts/departments?

- Do particular problems between functions continually surface?

- When problems do occur, what mechanisms exist to resolve them? How well do they work?

STEP FIVE: ASSESS THE SKILLS/KNOWLEDGE/ ATTITUDE REQUIREMENTS OF INDIVIDUALS

The final area of training needs analysis focuses on the requirements of individual employees. Information on current training needs can be gleaned from five main sources.

1 **Job descriptions/MBO format** What are the key job elements? Does the existing group of employees have the required knowledge/skills to complete their roles satisfactorily?

2 **Performance appraisal forms** where these highlight the development needs of the individual.

3 **Meetings with employees** Employees themselves are a key source of information on their own training needs. A meeting with an employee's manager, on the same subject, provides a degree of balance/objectivity to this data-gathering process.

4 **Direct observation** A skilful observer can often detect whether a job is being performed well or not.

5 **Organisational problems** If some activities continually pose a problem (e.g. reports are always late/poorly written, the level of customer complaints is high, sales targets are being missed etc.) this may highlight areas in which training may be useful.

These five sources will normally allow a diagnosis of current individual training needs to be completed. Well-constructed training programmes will then result in solutions, i.e. modified behaviour in which the "problems" experienced will be eliminated or substantially reduced.

A potential criticism here is that this focus is directing training through the "rear view mirror", i.e. too much emphasis on remedial/past practices. This can fairly easily be overcome by posing some "future requirements" questions.

► FUTURE TRAINING REQUIREMENTS

The future training needs of individual employees (often referred to as "development") may differ from current requirements for two reasons. Firstly, changes may be taking place in the environment (legislative updates/introduction of computerisation, etc.) which will require different knowledge/skill levels in the future (see earlier points made on this). Secondly, selected individuals (fast-track employees) may need to be groomed for future positions of greater responsibility. Where they exist, succession plans are an obvious source of information on your target group here.

► COLLECTING "TRAINING NEEDS" INFORMATION ON INDIVIDUALS

In practical terms there are a number of ways to collect data on individual training needs. These range from relatively simple (and quick) methods to self-audits and some fairly sophisticated instruments. Examples of each (ranging from simple to complex) are detailed in the following pages.

COLLECTING TRAINING NEEDS DATA: CAUSE CATEGORIES APPROACH

Before any decisions are made concerning the solution to a problem, we must determine why the problem exists. In relation to an identification of training needs, normally people do not perform for one or some combination of three basic reasons:

1 **Skill/knowledge problems** Employees don't know how, when or how well to perform. They don't know how, when or to what exact standard they are required to perform.

Example

A group of inexperienced sales clerks cannot write up sales slips. They don't know how, so this is a skill/knowledge problem.

2 **Environmental problems** People are prevented by the organisation or the environment by reasons other than skill or incentive deficiency.

Example

A group of sales clerks fail to write up sales slips during the Christmas rush. They know how, but the increased seasonal work load prevents them from performing — so this is an environmental problem.

3 **Motivation/Incentive problems** Employees are not motivated (lack incentive) to perform.

Example

A group of experienced sales clerks frequently do not write out sales slips. They know how, but don't want to because of a dispute with the company over commission payments — a motivation/incentive problem.

Possible Evidence of Skill/Knowledge Deficiency

You should suspect a skill/knowledge problem when some combination of the following is present:

1 Target population is new to the task.

2 Target population is generally low level in skills and knowledge.

3 Population has had no formal training in the task. History of inadequate training capability in the organisation.

4 Little attention paid at recruitment to match individuals and jobs.

5 No opportunity to practise skills while in training.

6 Training is "off-the-shelf" as opposed to being customised.

7 People cannot perform correctly even though they know they are being observed (or know their job depends on it).

Possible Evidence of Environmental Deficiency

You should suspect an environmental cause when:

1 There has been a history of some or all of the following:
   a Deadlines not being met.
   b Frequent management turnover.
   c Duplication of effort/poor work design.

2 There is no clear-cut chain of command or work flow.

3 Personnel have no alternative tasks to do while waiting on the product of some other person. Frequent appearance of personnel "not having anything to do".

4 Troubles with machines, lack of supplies, etc.

5 Some history of inter-group conflict (e.g. where performance of a task is dependent on others).

Possible Evidence of Motivation/Incentive Deficiency

You should suspect motivational/incentive problems when:

1 The deficient task is distasteful or socially negative.

2 The employee is unaware of the value of the products produced.

3 There is strong disagreement about the method that should be employed in performing the task.

4 The effort involved in performing the task is greater than the reward received.

5 Punishment is employed as the sole management technique.

6 Personnel do not get feedback on their work.

7 There is a history of documented motivational problems.

COLLECTING TRAINING NEEDS DATA:
SELF-AUDIT APPROACH

Under this heading the Training Manager normally asks employees to list the key skills or areas in which they need to improve. Some companies use a prepared listing of topics as a way to "prompt" this. One inherent danger in this approach is that it can become a "training menu" with items selected on the basis of "attractiveness" rather than being an identified training need (a well-designed questionnaire can overcome this — see Appendices M and N).

Typically, when you ask people to list their training or development needs, they will provide an open "self-audit". Similar to identifying training needs at the company level you should try to get "evidence" for the stated needs, e.g. problems in the current job, changing expectations for the future, etc.

Individual Level Analysis: Suggested Method for the Collection of "Training Needs" Data

The following is a suggested method for the collection of training needs data:

1 Get senior managerial support for your efforts. Overall, it is critically important that both the departmental manager and the individual employee "take ownership" for the training/development process. In helping them to assess training needs, you need to keep them in the loop rather than take over the process.

2 Gather as much "hard data" as possible (performance appraisal forms, sales vs. budgets, internal/external customer reports etc.) to give maximum background information/objectivity to your assessment.

3 Select the group of employees to be studied. Inform their manager of your purpose and set a time to meet them to explore training needs. Ask them to make some notes prior to your meeting on what they feel the key training needs (current problems/areas for future development) are for the selected employee(s). Alternatively, you can ask them to complete a Training Needs Questionnaire (see Appendices M and N).

4 Inform the individuals concerned and explain your purpose. Ask them to make some notes prior to your meeting (similar to those suggested for the managers).

5 At the meeting create a climate of openness by reassuring them that a listing of training/development needs is not a critique of current performance or abilities.

6 As far as you can, try to qualify the statements made against the data which you have collected/analysed.

7 As a final step you should establish a specific training objective, stated in behavioural terms. The identification of training needs is not an academic exercise. Results pay the bills and the training provided should have a measurable impact on organisational performance.

► BRIDGING THE GAP: THE SELECTION OF TRAINING METHODOLOGY

As a final stage, you should develop a listing of the possible methods to overcome the training/development needs. While "closing the training gap" is a separate subject area, often many training managers rely on too narrow a menu of possible solutions.

► HOW OFTEN SHOULD THE EXERCISE BE COMPLETED?

The Identification of Training Needs should be an annual process leading to the development of a total company "Training Plan". This will include sections on:

1 The external "context" in which the business operates

2 A summary of key issues facing the business

3 A listing of who needs training/and the specific training planned.

For practical purposes, half-way through the individual company performance planning cycle is probably the best time for this as the costs associated with the plan can be built into the forthcoming year's budgets.

MANAGING CHANGE:
THE DOUG MEYER CASE

▶ 9ᴛʜ DECEMBER: IF THE CAP FITS

Doug Meyer, the new President of Sterling Winthrop USA, looked out over the intersection of 40th Street and Lexington Avenue. Winter had finally arrived. The streets in New York were a moving sea of long over-coats, gloved hands and briskly walking people. In just over two hours it would snow again.

Tension filled the fifth-floor conference room. No one spoke. The stillness was almost painful. After an inde-terminate silence, Meyer restated the point, this time more forcefully: 'Look, if I have difficulty opening the cap, it must be really difficult for some of our cus-tomers".

The offending bottle of Bayer Aspirin lay in the centre of the table. By design it could only be opened by lin-ing up an arrow on the cap with an indentation on the bottle. Simple really. If you knew what to do. John Timony, Manufacturing Director for the Division, took up the argument.

"There are other issues here, Doug. Safety caps are a feature of all pharmaceutical packaging for two rea-sons. Firstly, medicines are dangerous. Safety pack-aging ensures that the risks of inappropriate usage, say, for example, by children, are minimised. Secondly ..."

"Please go ahead."

"... the entire pharmaceutical industry received a tremendous scare after the Tylenol incident, when cyanide was injected into the product. Since then the use of child-proof caps and safety seals has become standard and it is now regulated by the FDA."

Meyer took a moment to phrase the reply carefully: "I

accept the points made, John, but why can't we move to the industry standard, a "push down and twist" cap? It is much easier to open than our current design and still meets all the criteria you've listed."

"With respect, Doug, the cost of redesign and retooling is astronomical. We've looked at it before. We're talking a million dollars here."

This latter point found support in the assembled group. "I agree. In some ways this is a non-issue. We will be moving to glass bottles soon and the ..."

Meyer sat upright in his chair in what was becoming an increasingly tense moment for him. In many ways this meeting had come too early in his tenure. He would have liked to have had more time, built stronger bridges, reinforced more current initiatives. But ... "I hear what you are saying but cannot agree. As I see it, there are two fundamentals in this business, Quality and Customer Service. By staying with this packaging, we are in violation of both of these principles. We are going to change the cap design on the Bayer Aspirin product. That's the decision. Now I need you all to help me figure out how to do it."

The meeting broke up shortly afterwards. The mood was, at best, uncomfortable. Despite his initial expression of support for the team, words about respecting the past, Doug Meyer had taken a particularly strong stance, indeed had "pulled rank", on the Bayer caps issue. This guy was really hard to read. Was this an ominous sign of things to come?

Two months later all the engineering work had been completed. "Push down and twist" caps were in place on all Bayer Aspirin bottles. Doug Meyer had arrived.

JANUARY 1991: GACCIONE RESIGNS: AMBIGUITY RULES OK!

In North America Sterling Winthrop manufactured and marketed consumer health products under the divisional name Glenbrook Laboratories. In January 1991 Rich Gaccioni, President of the division, left the company to head up the consumer health business for Bristol-Meyer.

At that time Bristol-Meyer had a $600 million business versus $270 million for Glenbrook Laboratories. However, the increased job size was only part of the attraction. A recent reorganisation within Sterling Winthrop had changed five separate, and largely autonomous, divisions into two lines (Pharmaceutical and Consumer Health). In the new scenario, Gaccioni found himself reporting to an ex-peer. The greater opportunity (and purportedly higher salary) at Bristol-Meyer plus the reorganisation at Sterling Winthrop helped to make his decision to leave the company.

The search for a replacement candidate began immediately. Several internal people were considered for the post. Some of the high-potential internal candidates had only recently moved into "new" slots and the timing of a major promotion was poor; it was simply too soon. Some of the candidates within the particular division may also have suffered against the backdrop of a poorly performing business. The two major over-the-counter products, Bayer Aspirin and Phillips Milk of Magnesia, were both in a sales and share of market decline (Bayer held a 7 per cent share, down from a historical high of 40 per cent; Phillips was at 9 per cent, down from a high of 12 per cent). Despite the popularity of some internal candidates and an espoused company value of "growing its own timber", the search commenced for an external candidate to create a paradigm business shift.

Working through Gould and McCoy, an Executive Search firm in New York, Sterling Winthrop began a trawl of likely candidates. The pharmaceutical industry is small and many of the potential candidates were already known. Unfortunately, the business problems at Sterling Winthrop were also open knowledge in the industry. The market knew the company was "hurting"; there was no simple business solution to ageing brands which had little efficacy differentiation. If the North American market could be turned around it would not be "as a result of low-hanging fruit".

▶ MOVES AFOOT AT COLGATE PALMOLIVE

The imposing corporate offices of Colgate-Palmolive stand at Park Avenue in Manhattan. Within this huge corporation, Doug Meyer had steadily moved through a classic marketing career. After several successful positions, including a recent stint as Marketing Director in the UK, Meyer had returned to the US as Vice President of a new stand-alone oral care division.

▶ THE TOOTHPASTE LEAGUE TABLE

In the USA, the top position in the "toothpaste league" was held by Procter & Gambles' Crest. At the time Colgate-Palmolive were in number two position, holding a 17 per cent share with their Colgate brand. Between September 1988 and December 1990, under Meyer's direction, Colgate-Palmolives' share of the toothpaste market climbed steadily from

17 per cent to 33.5 per cent. In addition to the market share growth, the company successfully repositioned itself in "oral care" (a broader category definition) with the launch of the Colgate Plus toothbrush and the move into professional dentistry products. However, while the business was going exceptionally well, Meyer was becoming increasingly unhappy in the company.

Some time earlier, during 1989, Colgate-Palmolive had hired a new President. Almost immediately, the company underwent a change in core philosophy. In simple terms, the focus of the new regime was towards maximising operating profits rather than growing market share. During a strategic reorganisation driven by cost containment logic, efforts were made to pull the Oral Care unit back into the mainstream business, with a subsequent loss of autonomy for Meyer.

By early 1991 Meyer was considering both an international move with Colgate-Palmolive and a corporate global marketing position in New York, neither of which was fully satisfactory. In June 1991, he received a call from Bill Gould, the Executive Search Consultant working for Sterling Winthrop, and the long courtship dance which so often accompanies senior appointments commenced.

 ## TAKING THE PLUNGE: MEYER SIGNS UP FOR STERLING WINTHROP

From Meyer's perspective, the job with Sterling Winthrop offered a number of distinct benefits.

- It was a "line" rather than a staff job; Meyer definitely saw himself as a direct line manager type.

- It offered a "business turnaround" challenge. In his own words: "Where is the fun in taking over a successful company. All you can hope to do is not screw it up".

- 90 Park Avenue (the Sterling Winthrop Headquarters) was just ten blocks from his old job. In terms of making a career move it had the least possible negative disruption on his family.

- It was a full "President" title (he had earlier held both Vice President and General Manager titles in Colgate-Palmolive).

Mentally he worked down through the list. The more he thought about it the more it made sense. Yet the deciding factor may have been less rational than emotional. "Bayer", Sterling Winthrop's flagship product, was a household name and commonly used product in Meyer's own family. During the interviews he had been challenged by Kyle Greer, Sterling Winthrop's Director of Human Resources, to "restore the Bayer name to greatness".

Could he do it? It was certainly a major life decision to walk away from nineteen years of successful service and put himself as the "new boy on the block" at Sterling Winthrop. Meyer called Bill Gould and accepted the job. The start date was confirmed as October 1st, 1991.

 ## THE INTERIM MODE: MANAGEMENT BY COMMITTEE

Between January 1991 and October 1991, the Glenbrook Laboratories Division was run by the executive team who had formerly reported to Rich

Gaccione. In the absence of a divisional president, Herb McKenzie (then President of the world-wide Consumer Health Group), held direct responsibility.

Herb McKenzie had come from the old Sterling International division, the "golden children" within the company. The international division had had a lot of success in recent years. McKenzie, a fair but very tough manager by almost any standards, took it as a personal mission to "fix the problems in Glenbrook".

The Glenbrook management team was "shell shocked" for a number of reasons. Firstly, the previous management regime was somewhat more "gentlemanly"; the team were not fully aware that anything was "broken" and in need of being "fixed". Secondly, McKenzie's initial drive was to secure improved profitability with business growth a clear second objective, a reversal of their previous focus. Thirdly, McKenzie put a huge emphasis on having a "solid kitchen cabinet"; a series of lengthy and very probing meetings (the group met almost daily during this period) were held to "put the business back on the rails". Not for the first time in organisational history had a group been built on the basis of a perceived external threat to their professionalism. In 1991, the business had its first good year in over five consecutive years, with positive results recorded each quarter.

At the budget meeting in September, Herb McKenzie praised the Glenbrook management team for their great turnaround performance. It was an important watershed in the group's history. The nine months without a president, with McKenzie in the driving seat, had led to a strong bonding. It would not be easy for any outsider to dovetail with this team.

▶ OCTOBER '91 LOCK-ON: MEYER JOINS STERLING WINTHROP

In October 1991, Doug Meyer joined as the President of the renamed Sterling-Health, USA. In many ways he was not the "perfect fit". Meyer had spent all of his working life in Colgate-Palmolive. Within the pharmaceutical industry, nineteen years in the same company was deemed more negative (on the basis of "narrow experience") than positive (a plus on company loyalty). However, within Colgate-Palmolive his career progress and international experience overcame any "on paper" lack of breadth.

Through contacts in the industry, Meyer had already discovered that the sales team at Sterling Winthrop rated excellently. Their achievements (in terms of shelf facings, general relations with customers, etc.) were deemed superior to many competitor companies — even those who outwardly seemed to have a competitive edge, based on product spread, discounting policies etc. It was a solid foundation which could be built on; Meyer made a mental note.

▶ THE FIRST 100 DAY STRATEGY

The notion of the "first 100 days" as a particularly significant time for a new leader was dramatically publicised during the Bush-Clinton presidential transition. Meyer, quietly, began to prepare his own entry strategy. He had had some coaching. During the selection process the point had been stressed by Lou Mattis, President and CEO of Sterling Winthrop, that "maintenance of the status quo" would not be deemed successful; a slow "evolution" back into positive numbers followed by incremental business growth would not suffice.

Having observed many "new leaders" in Colgate-Palmolive, Meyer knew that the "everything-that-happened-in-the-past-is-wrong-this-is-the-way-it's-going-to-be" stance was a sure-fire method to lose the loyalty of the existing team. He had an informal inventory of "entry strategies" which he had seen work well in the past, including some personal mistakes. A former boss had counselled: "British people are not Americans. Talk softer. Be less blunt. Take it step-by-step".

The stint in the UK had taught him that a missionary zeal strategy could be inappropriate; the typical analytical British stance was often superior, or at least a good counter-weight, to his own natural sense of urgency. The dilemma faced here was how to make an entrance which clearly communicates "I've arrived" while at the same time ensuring you do not upstage the existing players. Not an easy one to call.

▶ MAKING AN ENTRANCE: DAY 1 AND DAY 2

During the first two days, Doug Meyer spent almost all of his time simply meeting the people in his group at 90 Park Avenue (both small group meetings and a general meeting with all staff in the centre of the office floor). It was a conscious and deliberate effort to market himself as a "real person" consistent with his view of himself as "basically an honest, good guy".

Dave Mahder, Vice President for Marketing, remembers the meetings and their impact: "He spoke about his kids, his house, the extended family heritage, and politely asked the same type of questions in return. It took a lot of guts. There was no pretension, no mystery, everything was on the table. It was the most authentic and most effective 'new boss' introduction I had ever seen."

Meyer consciously worked the 5th floor (Sterling Health, USA) and resisted the temptation to visit the 39th (where the Corporate Executive Group hang their hats), a feature which was to define his management style. "The best form of politicking is delivering the results. Results come through your people. Work well with your people and the rest will follow."

In similar vein he later remarked: "Ultimately it does not work. People see through it. Results are tangible, measured. Politicking is, at best, a very short-term gain. I'm not interested in Pyrrhic victories."

While few senior executives (who survive) could be described as apolitical, Meyer made it known that he did not wish to use politics as a success vehicle for himself or wish others who worked with him to focus too much on this.

 ## AT THE COALFACE: DAY 3 AND DAY 4

On days three and four in Sterling Winthrop, Meyer moved into the field — completing store checks in Chicago and Philadelphia with the sales force. It was a long time since the divisional president had spent time doing store checks; the grapevine went into overdrive.

The event, in part consciously designed to win the "hearts and minds" of the sales team, had an immediate positive impact. One of the senior executives commented: "It sent a really great message to the group. It gained Doug instant recognition and respect. It also generated a big 'to do' list. This guy was really listening and that's a consistent style to this day."

As another person later colourfully described it: "The interest of the new President was the business, not the bullshit. Anyone who goes into the field in his first week, is OK in my book. He got my vote straight away."

WHEN IS A BEAR NOT A BAYER?

Prior to Meyer's appointment, a new commercial for Bayer Aspirin had been developed. The advertisement featured a bear suffering from a headache. On taking a Bayer tablet, happiness was restored! The "Bear on Bayer" theme seemed a particularly clever word play. Despite objections from the legal team (concerned about copyright issues on the name), the marketing group were psyched on the commercial; it simply needed sign-off approval.

During the second week in the new job, Meyer was shown the commercial. His instinctive reaction was negative on the basis that it promoted a happy association with the Bayer name but did little to differentiate the product in terms of efficacy. He was now faced with a central dilemma. Should he throw his support behind a commercial he was personally uncomfortable with in order to show solidarity with his team? Or should he be honest, state the reasons underlying his feeling of discomfort and try to work out something different (a key problem here is that a commercial is the visual realisation of a concept; if the basic concept is flawed …).

As part of his "entry strategy", Meyer had made a conscious decision to support the existing team in what they were doing. While many new managers "critique the past", his own experience with this was that it alienated the incumbent group. Better to understand and honour the past and make changes slowly (speed is a relative term; in this particular business environment it probably meant making changes over some months rather than weeks). It is always easier to "push with the river"; psychology rule 101 states that you have to take a group from where they are now rather than where you want them to be. In what Meyer described as a "get on the train" philosophy, he decided to support the "Bear" commercial.

Later that week a preview of the new commercial had to be given to Lou Mattis, President and CEO of Sterling Winthrop. Despite a positive, upbeat presentation from the USA team led by Meyer, Mattis did not like the commercial. The marketing team asked for a month's breathing space to produce an alternative (there was a tremendous time constraint as TV space had been bought and the trade was promised a new commercial). One month later an alternative (known internally as the "colours" commercial) was produced and passed the various sign-off hurdles.

 ## OVERCOMING ADVERSITY: A PRODUCT OF OUR PAST?

Meyer is the youngest of two brothers who grew up in Scarsdale, Westchester County, a thirty-minute train ride north from Manhattan. Scarsdale, sometimes labelled "the richest town in the USA", is not short of high achievers — or their offspring. With an extremely intelligent elder brother and three academic cousins (who lived locally), Meyer's peer group set the bar high.

Surrounded by high academic achievers, Meyer found his forte in American football and baseball and began

The quality of a person's life is in direct proportion to their commitment to excellence regardless of their chosen field of endeavour

Vince Lombardi

to differentiate himself on the basis of physical prowess. Whether to overcome these early peer pressures or as a feature of some innate drive, his early and continuing life was marked by a strong need for achievement.

Graduating from high school with a very respectable 87 score (the Scarsdale High School "average" was 90), Meyer went to university and blossomed in economics. College led to graduate school and eventually an MBA.

During the second term in college, the then 23-year-old Meyer took a summer job in Colgate-Palmolive. He did not realise then that it was to be the start of a long relationship with the company. The MBA was completed at night, as Meyer cut his milk teeth in marketing. A series of business successes since that time led to the development of a personal style which was positive, upbeat and confident with little fear of making difficult judgement calls.

 CREATING AN ENVIRONMENT WHERE FAILURE IS ACCEPTABLE

In his first couple of weeks at Sterling Winthrop, three recurring themes were communicated both verbally and behaviourally:

• Meyer had a strong bias for action

• He had little time for formal organisation structure or convention

• He continually emphasised job security to create a climate under which people would turn around the results.

MAKING THE EFFORT: A BIAS FOR ACTION

One of Meyer's personal values is that failure based on genuine effort is acceptable; if you never fail you never try and this is unacceptable. One of his favourite stories concerns Babe Ruth, the great baseball player. A little-known fact is that in 1927, the year that Babe Ruth led the league in home runs (a record 60, which has never been surpassed) he also led in strike outs. The clear moral of the story was that strike outs are acceptable — as long as you are "swinging the bat". "I came here to swing the bat. Not having a clue about this business allowed me to swing and miss. The same goes for everyone around here."

FLAT STRUCTURES: UPWARD INFORMATION FLOW

A second element of Meyer's management style was the fact that he continually talked to people at all organisation levels. He is naturally gregarious, a living model of the MBWA (Management By Wandering Around) concept. A folksy "Hey – I'll take help wherever I can get it" or "I never resent anyone arguing with me, I resent it when they don't" is the outward expression of a thirst for knowledge about the business — from everyone at every level. Meyer used this time to collect nuggets of business information and attempted to piece these, jigsaw-like, into an overall whole. A clear understanding of "what you don't know" is a particularly useful, if scarce, commodity. However, the attempt at "closeness", coming as it did from an extremely well-dressed, loud-voiced individual was a little intimidating for some people.

Adding to the confusion, Meyer consciously positioned himself as playing two roles. Firstly, that of Doug Meyer, the marketer, the participant in group discussions, the team member; secondly, that of President, Sterling Winthrop, USA. In the early days people found it difficult to respond to this, to understand which hat he was wearing and the dual role notion caused some initial confusion. One thing was certain. It was not easy to "box" this guy neatly in any of the conventional categories.

PEOPLE CHANGE FROM A POSITION OF MEDIUM SECURITY

When a new manager joins a business which has not been performing well, it is almost inevitable that fears exist around job security. Meyer made a lot of effort to reassure people on this. "I did not come here to fire anyone. I had no illusions about being good enough to run this business on my own. I needed their help."

The stance was based on an unarticulated, yet extremely perceptive, understanding of human nature. Change and uncertainty create ambiguity. Remove people's security and they focus on CYA strategies, politicking and endless discussion and deliberations of the "what ifs"; it is an adult version of removing a child's comfort blanket. In the meantime, no one focuses on the business, except the competition! Creating insecurity is a sure way to deflect the available time onto non-productive issues and Meyer made strong initial efforts to assure people that his job was to "restore the business" rather than look for scapegoats for past efforts.

Despite the verbal assurances, it was to take more than six months for people to believe this and accept that there were not going to be wholesale cuts in the existing guard.

SCULPTING THE VISION: THE FLORIDA MEETING

Meyer's third week in office coincided with a long-planned strategic framework meeting which was held in Amelia Island, Florida. The strategic framework is a business planning and employee involvement process which sets the "strategic direction" for the company and details the operational requirements to ensure that this is achieved. Forty-five of the senior staff from Sterling Health, USA attended the meeting.

At the time the various elements of the strategic framework process (mission statement, goal areas, objectives, strategies and action plans) were new to Meyer; the mechanics of the meeting to debate/draft a "new framework" seemed somewhat confusing and almost "clumsy". In particular, it seemed that an inordinate amount of time was being spent "wordsmithing" and not enough on bold strokes; the "means" to business achievement (the strategic plan) seemed to be becoming an end in itself.

The meeting moved along for a couple of days, with sub-groups painstakingly piecing the elements of the jigsaw together. Although new to Sterling Winthrop, Meyer well understood the almost religious zeal with which the strategic framework was regarded and was reluctant to be critical of the construction process. However, he felt a growing sense of unease.

On day three the group was working in a large, U-shaped conference hall. In a move which could best be described as "part fact, but mostly faith", Meyer announced to an (at first) stunned audience that their strategic goal should be to build a half-billion dollar business by 1997. This represented an enormous 14 per cent compound growth rate over the five-year planning period, an outrageous target. Whether the enthusiasm of Meyer, the significance of the half-billion figure (or simply the heat of the Florida sun), the figure was embraced by the group. This marked a crucial turning point in the meeting, which became much more up-beat, positive and optimistic. "If this guy was prepared to put himself 'out on a limb', well maybe it could be done."

Later that evening Meyer was speaking on the phone with his line boss Herb McKenzie.

"How's the meeting going?"

"Great Herb. Really great. Earlier today we set a five-year vision of a half-billion dollars turnover."

"You what?"

"Yes, we put down our marker as a half-billion dollar turnover by 1997."

Herb, himself well known within the company as a past master of "bold strokes", was delighted. But even he was somewhat taken aback by the sheer magnitude of the growth. He asked, tentatively: "Can you do it, Doug?"

While the effort to paint bold strokes was laudable from a leadership perspective, in retrospect was it naive to set such a high target and internal expectations? The reply, another well thought out element of the Meyer philosophy: "Personally, I seldom think in terms of incremental improvement. (laughing) I'm a Quantum Leaper. In some ways big jumps are often easier than single steps."

Within four weeks of the meeting's end, the group had developed an "upside strategic plan" of $600,000; the half billion dollars vision had become a "floor" rather than a "ceiling" of achievement.

MAKING HISTORY: THE LAUNCH OF BAYER SELECT

In the middle of every difficulty lies opportunity

Albert Einstein

Bayer Aspirin is the flagship product of Sterling Winthrop, USA. At sales of $148 million in 1991, the product represented 47 per cent of total sales. In terms of importance to the company's success, it mirrored the marketing phrase, "the wonder drug that works wonders".

The brand, acquired in 1918 after the First World War repatriations, was suffering from tremendous competition in the analgesic category from competitor brands (Tylenol and Advil) and from generic aspirin (500mg of generic aspirin sells for $1.25 in drugstores across the USA; an equivalent quantity of Bayer Aspirin costs $4.00).

In 1987, the Bayer brand had received a sales boost through a number of clinical studies which had linked the taking of aspirin with the prevention of second heart attacks. The FDA (Federal Drug Administration) approved the claim to this effect. Within Sterling Health, Herculean marketing efforts were made to capitalise on this theme. A brilliantly executed advertising programme (one commercial showed a father at the birth of his son/daughter using the theme "Be around to see major events in your life") and the brand showed tremendous growth during this period. However, after two years the rush to self-medicate had subsided; without positive ongoing medical reinforcement, sales subsided. The brand had ridden the wave of a consumer health fad which had crashed. By the end of 1990, there was little doubt that the brand was in serious, long-term decline. The only light seemed to lie outside the aspirin market.

 BREAKING OUT OF THE ASPIRIN MARKET

Things may come to those who wait, but only the things left by those who hustle

Abraham Lincoln

The attempt to enter the non-aspirin market was not new. In 1982 an attempt had been made to launch Panadol, a paracetamol-based product which is a major brand for Sterling Winthrop in several international territories. Playing off its British heritage (the product was first launched in the UK in 1955), the advertisements ran against a backdrop of Big Ben in London. Another commercial played the angle of "world proven", showing footage from Holland and Australia, both of which are industrialised, advanced and would appeal to the typical USA consumer. The launch flopped without denting the market. After 12 months the company folded its tent and the campaign was discontinued. An expensive, painful lesson with regard to the North American market.

In relation to Bayer, internal debates around re-positioning, advertising execution, effective distribution and pricing had continued unabated for some time. Despite many valiant individual initiatives, brand sales were currently flat and in long-term decline. A critical internal debate centred on the concept of line-extension to capitalise on the existing brand equity with consumers.

One internal group argued strongly in favour of line extending the Bayer name, arguing that the major competitor product, J&J's Tylenol, had successfully extended its original pain relief equity (to include coughs and colds etc.). Another group argued that line extensions provide short-term sales growth at the expense of long-term positioning. The consumer's mind (the argument runs) is already hopelessly cluttered with brand information. By line extending a brand you run the risk of losing an established "positioning" in the consumer's mind and, over time, losing the equity. Part of the dilemma (or the magic, depending on your perspective) is the fact that there are no right or wrong answers; shades of grey abound.

In broad terms it had already been decided to move out of the aspirin market and to do some work on existing packaging. While these were "givens", the strategic direction for the Bayer brand had not been decided and the debate moved back and forth between the two camps.

As a newcomer to the business, Meyer felt that the analgesic category was hopelessly confused. A visit to any local drugstore was a lesson in pharmacology. For the relief of mild pain, consumers had a choice of Aspirin, Paracetamol and Ibuprofen. Each individual brand stressed the benefits of the particular active ingredient; it was a sophisticated consumer indeed who could make an informed choice.

Within the marketing team a germ of a positioning strategy began to unfold. Could Sterling Winthrop capitalise on the confusion in the category by focusing on the *type* of pain which the consumer experiences rather than the remedy? The concept of "Bayer Select" slowly emerged. In a brilliant piece of innovative strategic marketing, the brand moved from being ingredient-specific to symptom-specific — allowing a range of formulas and active ingredients to be applied under the general Bayer umbrella (the slogan "all pain is not the same" was born and graphically captured the new positioning).

The concept launch was backed by the biggest advertising commitment ever made for any new consumer health product in North America, over $116 million in support efforts. The launch was due to begin in November 1992.

In many ways this was the real test, the big one. Sitting alone in his fifth-floor office, Doug Meyer kept his fingers crossed as he said a silent prayer.

10

EMPLOYEE TEAMS:
THE STERLING WINTHROP CASE

TEAMWORK IN ACTION

Employee Involvement Teams at Sterling Winthrop

Three and a half years ago, I did not want to come to work anymore. This has changed my life.

Packaging Operator

In order to avoid being buried tomorrow, we need to create space today.

Tom Berry, Plant Manager

We needed to get new forming dies. The total cost for the new dies was $50,000. We figured that reconditioned dies were the answer and put the whole proposal together. They eventually cost $6,000, that's a saving of $44,000, and we did it ourselves.

Plant Operator

We have an input here. The managers actually ask us what we think. Most places where I worked previously you were told, but you were never asked.

Packaging Operator

▶ MAHAFFY ONE AND MAHAFFY TWO

The afternoon of November 17th, 1992 was cold and heavily overcast. Little light penetrated the vertical windows which dotted the flat, exterior wall of the plant's canteen. Above the entrance door an electronic "ticker tape" flashed the five company values in sequence — We Are A Winning Team, We Are Customer Driven, We Have A Sense Of Urgency, We Are Dedicated To Continuous Improvement, We Act Responsibly. The value messages were interspersed with welcome greetings to plant visitors.

In the far corner of the canteen a set of four tables were arranged in a perfect square. Just after 3 p.m. people began to filter in slowly. A group of eight took up position at the arranged tables. Notebooks and catalogues were silently opened.

When all the members had arrived, two different conversations started almost immediately. One sub-group discussed a method to cut "strips" (plastic ties which hold incoming materials onto delivery pallets); left long, they were a trip hazard. The second group discussed the setting up of an additional 5cc packaging line. They were agreed: another line would significantly speed up the existing process. Midway through the meeting the topic of using different coloured worktops was discussed. These would make it much easier to detect product defect patterns (the varying coloured labels on some products make it difficult to spot errors when a fixed colour background is used).

The intense discussions were punctuated by some good humoured "ribbing" and banter. The pace was fast. Twice members left the group, without announcement, to seek additional information. On return the information was shared; a decision reached, the group moved on.

Lots of separate activities were underway simultaneously. One woman completed a report; another flicked through a manufacturer's catalogue comparing pricing on packaging equipment; a third filled the role of "team leader", helping to facilitate the group by constantly asking questions and drawing out individual members' opinions. Some subtle training of peers was also taking place: "What exactly is in that SOP (standard operating procedure)?" "No problem. Here's how it works ..."

Just before 4.00 p.m. the unmistakable signs of the meeting ending began to take place. As silently as they had come, the group filed out and returned to their respective packaging lines. Mahaffy One and Mahaffy Two were back in production.

► EMPLOYEE INVOLVEMENT TEAMS IN ACTION

A production management team meeting? An engineering group trying to reconfigure the process? The Plant Safety Committee in action? Right? Wrong on all counts. Simply a group of production operators engaged in an Employee Involvement Team at Sterling Winthrop's McPherson Plant in Kansas, USA.

Employee Involvement Teams (normally referred to as EITs) are groups of direct production employees who use their own expertise and resources to improve performance and upgrade the quality of work life. They perform aspects of roles which in traditional manufacturing plants are the territory of purchasing managers, safety officers, QA inspectors, supervisors, facilitators, secretaries, expeditors, technicians and industrial engineers. At McPherson, change is not negotiated or resisted but embraced and accepted as a constant — without any additional pay or extrinsic reward; and people there are completely enthused by the process, animated, active, positive, committed. It is indicative of the level of trust in the plant that a complete stranger (with a very non-Kansas accent) could join their meeting — without any visible sense of self-consciousness or apprehension by the group. After a very courteous welcome, I was politely ignored while the business at hand was tackled.

HOW THE EMPLOYEE INVOLVEMENT TEAMS SYSTEM WORKS

Employee Involvement Teams are groups of employees who normally work together in defined areas. At the present time, there are 63 teams in operation throughout the plant and participation is mandatory for all personnel. Groups are small (six to eight members is typical). Meetings are held between 7.30 and 8.30 on Tuesday mornings (by exception, some groups hold their meetings at a different time e.g. to facilitate on cross-over with second shift personnel in the afternoon).

The perceived value of the one hour per week (a 2.5 per cent time expenditure) is that it is one hour of "strategic time" in a sea of "operational time". Having a distinct time allocation encourages people to review critically "where they are now" and concentrate on eliminating non value-added work in the existing process.

During 1992 three themes (Productivity, Quality and Safety) were announced and all Employee Involvement Teams directed to focus on these. Using these general themes for direction, the groups self-select particular projects to work on. Not uncommonly, groups have a couple of projects running side by side. Many of the teams keep a whiteboard near their work area to capture ideas; when the current projects are completed, they move onto these. If technical expertise is required on any aspect, the groups recruit this within the plant, simply by asking the relevant person to help out. Where process changes are suggested the teams normally work the proposed method on a trial basis.

A specific form is used to record all Employee Involvement Team meetings. The forms are reviewed monthly by the Plant Manager after the scheduled meetings, which helps him to keep abreast of developments and acts as a visible sign of continued managerial support.

TRAINING AND DEVELOPMENT: PROVIDING THE TOOLS

Each of the Employee Involvement Team members has been trained in problem-solving/decision-making skills by the American Quality Management Institute. This covers the usual range of diagnostic tools (Fishbone Charting, Affinity Diagrams, Scatter Diagrams, Pareto Charts, Brainstorming etc.). The training in the use of these tools has a primary benefit of skills-building and a secondary benefit of confidence development. For some operations personnel, it has been many years since they attended formal school and they have to be "retrained", both to critically evaluate what currently exists and to understand that such criticism is totally legitimate in the McPherson environment.

RECOGNITION SYSTEM: TELLING THE GOOD NEWS

Each month, five Employee Involvement Teams are selected randomly and their work is recognised. Information from the teams is posted on a dedicated notice board in the cafeteria. Other groups review the board and there is tremendous cross-pollination of ideas.

MANAGERIAL SUPPORT: A CRITICAL FACTOR

If the expenditure level is large (above $500) the teams prepare their own completed Staffwork Reports to get the required support. The credibility of the system is high because of the level of overt managerial support for items requested. "The vast majority of requests get the green light. If something gets shot down it's usually because we have overlooked some element or there may be something happening in parallel which we are not aware of."

Over time, teams are given and have come to expect more autonomy: "Our team needed to work overtime. We decided to work an extra hour per day rather than on Saturday. It worked out fine."

An intriguing sub-benefit of this level of autonomy is that the teams work indirectly on "teamwork" issues; two instances were cited where the teams helped individual members come to terms with a productivity norm (both cases resolved successfully). Here, a contentious element of the traditional supervisory role is managed directly by the team (the supervisory team is still largely intact, although many of the functions traditionally associated with the supervisory role are now performed by the Employee Involvement Teams).

UNDERSTANDING THE CONTEXT: THE McPHERSON PLANT

McPherson is a small town of 12,000 people located almost at the exact centre of Kansas — and at the geographical heart of the USA. The town and county of McPherson bear the name of civil war General James Birdseye McPherson who was killed in the Battle of Atlanta in 1864. Most of the county's early settlers were farmers lured from the east by the promise of free land. The farming tradition and the strong work ethic which accompanied this are still very much in place in McPherson today.

On the treeless plains of central Kansas, the Sterling Winthrop plant in McPherson, a 263,000 square foot manufacturing facility, is the second largest employer in the town. The plant employs just over 400 salaried (non-union) people. McPherson was selected as a location after consideration was given to a number of sites (tax rates, infrastructure, wage rates, industrial relations and local salaries all being weighted in the decision process).

STERILE PRODUCTS: HUGE VOLUMES

The plant was built in the mid-1970s with the first batch of commercial product released in 1977. Products are all water-based injectable drugs manufactured in several configurations (ampoules, vials, bottles and disposable cartridges). The largest product in terms of units is the Carpuject disposable syringe.

In 1991, 83 million Carpuject units were produced and sold (sales for 1992 were forecasted to exceed 90 million units). Vial products represented the largest dollar volume at McPherson (bottle volume exceeds one million units per annum). Ampoules had shown steady performance over the last several years and were produced in the 17 to 18 million units per year range. The final product category is the Cook-Waite dental cartridge business. Five products under this heading were expected to sell 30 million units in 1992.

▶ THE MOVE TO QUALITY CIRCLES

The concept of employee involvement at the McPherson plant had been in steady evolution since the mid-1980s. The first stirrings began in 1980 with the establishment of several "Quality Circles" at the plant. Quality Circles (an outgrowth of the Japanese notion of "Kaizan" or continuous improvement) involved local work teams meeting on a regular (normally weekly) basis to discuss/resolve quality issues.

In keeping with the general theme of "participation" membership of the Quality Circles was voluntary. However, a practical problem soon arose. New work methods proposed by Quality Circle members could be vetoed by non-participants if they did not buy-in. As only 50 per cent of the workforce participated in Quality Circles, many initiatives proposed were not pursued. On the plus side, a strong foundation of problem-solving/decision-making skills training was laid with up to 200 people receiving skills training in problem-solving and decision-making.

Despite the fact that some positive progress was achieved, the structural negative of voluntary participation proved a definite burden. The concept slowed considerably; by 1985, there were few really active Quality Circles at the plant.

OMNIPAQUE PRODUCTION IS MOVED TO PUERTO RICO

The problem with the future is that it usually arrives before we are ready for it

Arnold H. Glasow

In 1986, a negative external threat initially energised the employee involvement concept. Under the US 936 Tax Law, manufacturers in Puerto Rico were allowed an effective tax rate of 4 per cent on company profits. The comparable rate in Kansas was approximately 32 per cent. Higher labour productivity rates at the Kansas plant could not overcome this structural difference in taxes as labour costs only represented 8 or 9 per cent of total product costs. In line with many other pharmaceutical manufacturers, Sterling Winthrop established a production facility in Puerto Rico and moved production of its flagship product, Omnipaque (a radio-contrast media) offshore.

The move led to a wave of uncertainty at the McPherson plant which proved to be a double-edged sword. On the plus side the threat to the plant's existence created a climate of uncertainty and acceptance of the need for change; there would be little resistance to management efforts to improve the plant's effectiveness if this translated to better job security. The downside was that in a climate of insecurity, the idea of employees coming together to "reduce waste, speed-up and question existing norms", was analogous to a turkey voting for Thanksgiving. Would productivity gains for Sterling Winthrop at the McPherson plant be at the expense of employees' jobs?

During this period, headcount at the plant fell from over 500 to under 400 people; employees were sceptical that the company really wanted them to participate in improving the plant's performance at a time when so many of their colleagues were losing their jobs. The local management team needed some mechanism to lift the spirits — a rallying cry to reactivate the enthusiasm and commitment of the workforce.

SUBVERSIVE LEADERSHIP

Tom Berry, then Production Manager, supplied the missing spark by appealing to the prevailing self-image. In Kansas, the tough, western spirit lives on. In a marvellous example of "subversive leadership", Berry told the people: "If we're going down, we are going down with our boots on. Not because we laid down and quit. If anyone from the east coast (a reference to the Corporate Group) thinks that the people in Kansas are wimps, they don't know the style here. We can compete with anyone, anywhere. This plant is a great plant and we will show the rest of the Sterling Winthrop world what we can do."

It was a fighting, spirited message. The group bought into it. The climate, in terms of a belief in the local ability to influence events, started to turn around; the idea of an effective participation structure was actively considered again.

A VISION OF WHAT COULD BE

At that time Berry was completing his Master's in

Management degree at Friends University in Wichita. He was impressed with cases detailing how companies had brought about positive change within adversarial trading environments. He was convinced that in order to survive, the McPherson plant needed to innovate constantly, push the quality ceiling higher and improve productivity. Faced with tough, internal competition the plant simply had to become "Better, Faster, Cheaper".

If you have always done it that way it is probably wrong

Charles Ketterin

Participation was key to this. In Berry's words: "People work a lot harder on something which is their idea, rather than something imposed. They want to have a personal stake in it."

FROM QUALITY CIRCLES TO EMPLOYEE INVOLVEMENT TEAMS

On September 20th, 1988, Berry wrote to John Durso, Vice President for Manufacturing, proposing the establishment of a formal system for employee involvement throughout the plant. Berry argued that in order for the programme to be successful, two points would be absolutely critical:

Faced with the choice between changing one's mind and proving that there is no need to do so, almost everybody gets busy on the proof

John Kenneth Galbraith

- It should be non-voluntary in order to embrace everyone in the plant (the solution: make participation mandatory).

- It must have senior management support (the solution: the senior management team at the plant was to become the Steering Group for the new Employee Involvement Teams).

Durso supported the proposal; Berry was given the green light to make it happen.

▶ MAKING IT HAPPEN: ENERGISING THE INFORMAL ORGANISATION

New ideas often initially need to have a cadre of supporters to overcome the natural inertia which exists in most organisations. Berry personally approached a number of people in the plant (some of whom had been outspokenly negative on the Quality Circles concept), explained the idea and asked for their support. The message was simple: "You're my guy. I want you on the team supporting this."

Apart from one or two people, most signed up and became lead players in the early stages of the Employee Involvement Teams. These "seed teams" were set up and spread like a "positive cancer" throughout the organisation.

▶ OVERCOMING RESISTANCE: GETTING THE SUPERVISORS ON BOARD

In January 1988, Berry was promoted to Plant Manager and immediately set out to put the Employee Involvement Teams system on a more formal footing. From reading and talking with other companies, he knew that the single biggest obstacle to successful Employee Involvement Programs often came at the supervisory level. Their reasoning is not difficult to understand. If the participation initiative results in productivity improvements, senior management usually have a definite, visible gain. Employees lower in the hierarchy usually have the benefit of additional involvement and participation. It is the supervisory group who potentially lose out as their traditional role and power base becomes eroded. Berry decided to use training as the key change lever.

The consulting group Peat Marwick had been assisting the company in implementing a Just-In-Time (JIT) system. They were asked to design a programme to "train the supervisors" to operate in the new environment. The programme had both educational elements ("here's what it is") and some skill-building ("here's what you need to do"). Most of the supervisors, seeing the potential benefits, accepted the new direction. However, some found it extremely difficult.

"You are telling me that I am a Coach, a Mentor. I don't even understand these terms. Do I not tell my people what to do anymore?"

"All my life, I have worked to get into a supervisory role. After working for 15 years, I've just made it last year. Now you're telling me the job no longer means anything."

▶ MAKING THE HARD CALLS: CHANGING THE OLD GUARD

Despite efforts to train, coach and continually sell the Employee Involvement Teams ideas (and the concepts which underlay this), some of the supervisory group could not "get on board"; the idea of losing their supervisory role was simply too much of a change, where becoming a supervisor had been a much sought after symbol. With great reluctance, five supervisors were eventually outplaced.

In Berry's words: "We were really trying to be fair, to the people and to their families. We did everything we possibly could, spending a lot of time with this group, individually and as a group. However, there was just too much momentum to let it stop."

*In a fight
between you
and the world,
bet on the world*

Frank Kafka

A harsh reality of organisations is "if you can't change the people, change the people". While the problem was mainly within the supervisory groups, one departmental manager left the company for similar reasons. Despite the fact that he intellectually understood the direction, he had never been emotionally committed to it. Under pressure, he would revert to a highly autocratic management style which was the antithesis of the espoused philosophy. His personal style simply was not suited to the new environment and he lacked the ability or the motivation to change.

The outplacement had a contradictory impact on the Employee Involvement Team programme. On the plus side it was a positive signal (in some ways the ultimate signal) of real managerial commitment to the concept. The downside was that it fuelled a mood of uncertainty/insecurity within the remaining supervisory group who were critical to its ongoing success. Berry and the senior management team spent a lot of time with this group, working through implementation difficulties with the Employee Involvement Teams concept. They wanted to underscore the value of the supervisors' expertise, most of whom had ten to twelve years' service. It was not until 1990, a full five years after initial commencement, that the programme could be said to be really in place and accepted by everyone in the plant.

EMPLOYEE INVOLVEMENT TEAMS: MEASURING THE IMPACT

Critics of the employee involvement doctrine argue that there is often little real business value in the approach. While the improvements in working life are broadly recognised, the argument runs that this seldom

The pure and simple truth is rarely pure and never simple

Oscar Wilde

translates into superior business performance. Does the commitment of one hour per week (2.5 per cent of available time) and the necessary managerial emotional expenditure represent good value for money?

Within Sterling Winthrop, the central measurement used for a manufacturing plant was operating variance. This reflects productivity against a fixed standard under the headings of direct labour, materials and overhead costs, measures which are normally tracked on a monthly basis. At the McPherson plant, the numbers suggested a strong correlation between improved business performance and the Employee Involvement Teams.

By the end of October 1992, the operating variance for McPherson was positive by $820,000 — with $950,000 projected for the full year. (During the same time period in 1991, the figure was $273,000). Primarily, these figures were achieved through labour productivity gains (improved quality, decreased overtime working, less product rework, reduced changeover times, less equipment downtime, etc). Manufacturing variances have been positive for a straight period of 28 months.

REJECT LEVELS ARE IN DECLINE

Rejects are measured as a percentage of parts per million (PPM). The current plant average (across all product lines) was 2 per cent, down from a 5 per cent average in 1990.

To understand the significance of these numbers, account has to be taken of the fact that the Profit Improvement Program (PIP) has been in place for 14 years. Under this programme an annual cost reduction target (5 per cent of cost of goods) is set. Central point:

Much of the "fat" had already been stripped out of the system. McPherson primarily manufactures "old" products (Demerol, Hypaque etc.) which had seen a minimum of 10 consecutive years of production standard improvements which absorbed price and labour cost increases. The productivity improvements noted therefore represent a real added value benefit which is in addition to this.

Yet a central difficulty remains: is it possible to establish that the existence of Employee Involvement Teams and the superior performance are directly linked? No causal relationship can be scientifically established (in the same way that the link between smoking and lung cancer cannot yet be medically "proven"). Some of the evidence is anecdotal. For example, the two areas of the plant where reject levels have not fallen so dramatically are also identified as areas where less effective supervision is in place. The bottom line is that there is no "smoking gun" direct evidence link between Employee Involvement Teams and superior plant performance. While this may seem, to some, a form of "conceptual looseness", the figures speak for themselves. In the final analysis, the strongest argument is probably provided by Tom Berry: "I don't really care what box or label we use. If we keep pushing the productivity up — we'll take it from wherever we can."

SELF-SELECTED PROJECTS TEND TO BE NARROWLY FOCUSED

Another potential criticism of an employee involvement system where teams work on self-selected projects is that it can miss the "big-hitters"; most quality problems are process design issues — within the ambit

*80% of all
quality problems
are within the
scope of
management's
resolve*

Edward Demming

of management control and often outside the scope of employees. Indeed, the vast majority of Employee Involvement Teams prefer to work on "boundaried" projects (short time span, within their scope of authority to bring about change) which narrows their potential impact. At the McPherson plant, they overcame this "small picture" argument by having a three-pronged project identification/selection structure:

• **The Strategic Framework:** Revised annually, this sets out the "key" issues to be addressed at the plant. It includes major process issues which have been identified as sources of potential quality problems. Individual managers take these as part of their MBOs.

• **Project Teams:** Cross-functional Project Teams have been established to tackle specific "big" projects (e.g. at the time of writing a team was overhauling the stability system; this team had been in place for more than a year and will continue to work for some time on this major project).

• **Employee Involvement Teams:** The argument that EITs focus on "narrow issues" is probably true initially. Most tend to focus on "Quality of Worklife"-type projects (making seating at the production line more comfortable, repainting work areas in different colours etc.), rather than productivity issues per se. Part of the reason here is that they simply want to feel a sense of success; smaller, boundaried projects provide the best opportunity for this. However, this tends to change as a team "matures" (after about 18-24 months of operation). Tom Berry argues: "We definitely see a change in the type of the issues tackled. Over time teams become more assertive, taking on 'riskier', longer-term projects. It is partly a function of growing confidence. Management must allow enough space, up front, for teams to work on 'their' agenda. People need to see that we will support them on this."

Through the above structural mechanisms, the potential argument that the involvement process only focuses on "small" issues is largely overcome.

EMPLOYEES' PERCEPTION OF THE INVOLVEMENT TEAMS

A potential downside for the employees involved is the increased responsibility faced. Along with authority comes responsibility and the whole baggage associated with this, including increased stress. A number of employees mentioned, quite independently of each other, that they often spent coffee/lunch breaks discussing work-related issues. Was the potential loss of personal time a cause of concern to the employees at McPherson? Not on the basis of the sample of people met during the construction of this case:

"The company are more honest in levelling with us now. It has definitely improved attitudes. It helps a lot."

"When you see the results, it pushes you to do better. It's really great here now."

"People work much more as a team and are more considerate to each other."

At the time of writing a major plant renovation, including the purchase of several new pieces of equipment, was underway. This underscores a visible commitment to the plant. In one person's words: "We are really on the map now. We feel we have a future here."

Part of the commitment is explained through a stronger feeling of job security; part through the human need to be listened to and treated with respect. Visits to the plant by divisional executives (not easily accomplished; door to door, it is a seven-hour plus trip from Manhattan) also signal the company's commitment to the plant. Several people at the plant were complimentary about executives taking the time to visit.

To use a marketing analogy we could ask what "share of market" does the Employee Involvement Team concept have? While there is no method in place to evaluate this scientifically, the consensus is that the vast majority of employees (over 85 per cent) are completely sold on the participative systems in place and would not wish them to be discontinued.

 INVENTING TOMORROW TODAY

Predictions are always difficult. Especially those about the future

Chinese Proverb

Not content with accomplishments to date, the management team are currently working through the literature on self-directed teams and speaking with a number of external companies. In Berry's words: "If we have a talent it is to listen and to steal good ideas."

Another layer of empowerment is theoretically possible, with groups performing the functions of recruitment, performance management/appraisal and even tackling discipline/dismissal issues. While all of this is for another day, there is no complacency within McPherson on what has been achieved to date and a healthy dissatisfaction with the status quo prevails.

Those who seek a simple "magic bullet" answer to raising employee morale and productivity will be disappointed by the McPherson story. The Employee

Involvement Teams are an overnight success story that has been seven years in the making — the result of tremendous, sustained managerial commitment and employee goodwill. The final shape of the McPherson plant employee involvement design remains to be written.

APPENDICES

VALUES: SEARCHING FOR THE EVIDENCE

Below is a listing of "value sources" which provide clues to what an organisation believes in.

LEADERSHIP SPEECHES	Leader's behaviour – Dealing with people – Use of time – Key messages in Annual Report – Time at Key Meetings?
INFORMATION STATISTICS	What is measured, tracked?
REWARDS	Material and symbolic; pay, advancement, inclusion, exclusion, praise …
USE OF SPACE	(e.g. Focus on teamwork, but you have to book a room for a group meeting) — access, location, size, layout, status, badges of rank.
PERSONNEL AND TRAINING POLICIES AND PROCEDURES	Investment in training, equality, etc.
BEHAVIOUR TOWARDS CUSTOMERS	"Customer is King" — but …
ORGANISATION STRUCTURE / AUTHORITY TO DECIDE	Empowerment, delegation …
ARTEFACTS	What are the visible signs …

B
THE STRATEGIC FOCUS PLAN EVALUATION TOOL

The following instrument provides you with a set of key questions against which you can "measure" your existing mission/vision/values etc.

Mission Statement Prework	Yes	?	No
1 Analysis of the market and specific identification of each of the market segments that constitute the target market.			
2 Identification of the needs of customers in each target market segment, and how those needs are met by the company's products and services.			
3 Analysis of existing competitors in each market segment — their strengths, weaknesses, and strategies.			
4 Assessment of value provided to customers by competing products and services.			
5 Assessment and probable impact on the industry and company of the significant issues in the external environment such as: • social trends, including buyer habits and lifestyles; • economic trends, including risks and opportunities; • political issues, including legislative and regulatory changes; • technological developments, including effects on customers, suppliers, and competitors, as well as the company itself.			
6 Analysis of how social and other trends will change existing market segmentation and customer needs.			

Mission Statement	Yes	?	No
1 Is clear and easy to read/understand.			
2 Is oriented primarily toward the company's customers rather than its owners.			
3 Is sufficiently unique to the company that it could not apply equally well to competitors; your company name could not simply be replaced by another company name.			
4 Expresses a noble purpose that staff will be proud to work towards.			
5 Describes the company's responsibilities to its various stakeholders.			
6 Describes a particular business domain/niche and why this is attractive.			
7 Identification of specific companies who are not now competitors but who may enter the marketplace and the reasons why they would do so.			
8 Analysis of the impact of free trade and deregulation.			
9 Identification of how technological developments will create new customer needs and new ways of fulfilling new and existing needs.			
10 Identification of threats and opportunities arising from developments in international markets.			

Company Vision	Yes	?	No
1 Is clearly derived from the organisation mission.			
2 Is not too closely aligned with any single individual.			

Company Vision (contd)	Yes	?	No
3 Sets a "stretch" goal to work towards that is challenging.			
4 Is worked in an emotive/exciting way; paints a clear "word picture".			?
5 Is developed by a broad group of internal personnel.			
6 Has a clear timeframe.			
7 Is translatable into key results/action plans.			
8 Is endorsed and frequently communicated by Senior Management.			

Company Values	Yes	?	No
1 Identifies Values which support the organisational strategy. Will help us to "win".			
2 Describes in clear terms the behaviours which will support the stated Values which employees can feel proud of. Stated Values are well expressed.			

Key Result Areas — Business Strategy	Yes	?	No
1 Highlights the distinctive capabilities that must be created to attain long-run competitive advantage.			
2 Identifies positions in relation to market share, profitability etc., that the company must occupy to maintain sustained long-term superior performance.			
3 Leads to concentration of efforts, e.g. are not too expansive.			

Key Result Areas — Business Strategy (contd)	Yes	?	No
4 Is consistent with the environment, competition and consumers.			
5 Fully exploits company strengths and opportunities/minimises threats.			
6 Chosen level of risk is realistic.			

Measurements	Yes	?	No
1 Can easily be used to measure performance/monitor progress.			
2 Are realistic and attainable.			
3 Are clear/easily understood.			

Implementation	Yes	?	No
1 Action plans exist to progress each of the key elements of the Strategic Focus Plan.			
2. All existing work/MBO's links with the "Focus Framework". Nothing is excluded.			
3 Employees clearly understand each of the elements and the rationale for these.			
4 Adequate resources are in place to accomplish the goals set.			

THE CUSTOMER IS KING QUESTIONNAIRE

Clear Vision	Yes	No	Don't Know
A clear vision of excellent customer service exists within our organisation			
Decisions made in the organisation are judged against their impact on customer service			
We have lots of artefacts (posters, quotes, sayings, photographs) on the theme of customer service			
We almost never participate in destructive comments about our customers			
All of our internal activities are designed to create value for our customers			

Identify Your Customers

Our external customers are clearly identified to everyone in the organisation			
We often visit our customers' organisation; our managers spend considerable time in the field to ensure that they understand our customers' needs			
Our external customers often visit our organisation			
The concept of internal customers is clearly understood within our organisation			

Understand your Customers' Needs	Yes	No	Don't Know
Formal systems are in place to ensure we understand our customers' needs			
Informal systems are in place to ensure we understand our customers' needs			
We maintain an active bank of customer-related information			
We try to anticipate our customers' needs			
The products and services we deliver are determined by our customers' needs			
Our customers' existing needs are understood			
We work really hard to understand the needs of internal customers			

Deliver the Product/Service

Our customers' needs determine the way we deliver products and services to them			
We are at the leading edge of technology usage in our industry			
We under-promise and over-deliver to our customers			
Our people are empowered to make customer-related decisions			
Our managers personally demonstrate a commitment to excellent customer service			
We provide excellent service to ALL our customers			

Measure to Verify Satisfaction Levels	Yes	No	Don't Know
We deliver on time/cost what we say we will			
Formal measurement systems are in place to verify the level of customer satisfaction			
Informal measurement systems are in place to verify the level of customer satisfaction			
We provide recognition to our customer service champions			
Customer satisfaction levels are communicated to everyone in the organisation			
Our customers are satisfied with their relationship with us			
Overall, we are truly a "customer-driven" company			

TESTING YOUR KNOWLEDGE OF OUTPUTS: EXERCISES

Use this case study to test your understanding of outputs. The case presents you with details on a particular company and challenges you to decide what constitutes inputs and outputs for people who have different roles within the company. In providing you with a solution, it gives you a yardstick against which you can measure your learning.

Read the case and complete the four exercises detailed on the following pages. Complete each exercise individually and check your answers before you move onto the next exercise. The correct answers are detailed on the final page of the Appendix.

▶ THE ATLANTIC INDUSTRIES CASE

Mr Paul Sinclair is owner and General Manager of Atlantic Industries Limited, manufacturers and distributors of wood furniture products. He founded the company, designed most of the products and is on friendly terms with most major customers. He walks through the plant every day and all workers call him by his first name.

Tables and chairs account for 89 per cent of the sales volume, split 40 per cent in industrial sales and 60 per cent in the household consumer market. Other products in the line include book cases, footstools, desks and similar types of cabinet work. A unique drying and finishing process developed by Mr Sinclair enables the use of native spruce, which is considerably cheaper in cost than other more traditional woods. Raw materials are purchased from several sawmills and shipments both in and out are mainly by road transport.

Approximately 70 individuals are employed by the firm, most of whom are utilised in the production process while four salesmen each sell the full line. An accountant and several clerks look after the paperwork.

Production is divided into three distinct phases — cutting, assembly and finishing. Although patterns, drawings and specifications are available for each product, the workmen are so familiar with the operations that they seldom refer to them.

Sales are made essentially in two ways: either through contacts with architects and builders, or to retail suppliers of household and industrial furniture.

▶ EXERCISE 1

The following outputs for the **Sales Managers** unit were considered. Three of them are "Outputs", mark them "O". Three are "Inputs", mark them "I". Two are probably outputs but should be moved horizontally or vertically as they appear to be someone else's responsibility, mark them "S".

A   Customer Relations ☐
B   Sales Costs ☐
C   Sales Levels ☐
D   Product Line Profitability ☐
E   New Customers ☐
F   New Product Development ☐
G   Advertising Policy ☐
H   Sales Force Motivation ☐

EXERCISE 2

The following outputs for the **Accountants** unit were considered: Four of them are "Outputs", mark them "O". One is an "Input", mark it "I". One is someone else's responsibility, mark it "S".

A   Management Information
B   Cost of Capital
C   Taxes
D   Cash Flow
E   Signing Cheques
F   Profit

EXERCISE 3

The following outputs for the **Plant Managers** unit were considered. Three of them are "Outputs", mark them "O". Two are inputs, mark them "I". Two are someone else's responsibility, mark them "S".

A   New Customers
B   Manufacturing Cost
C   New Products
D   Quality
E   Plant Utilisation
F   Machine Maintenance
G   Hiring Employees

EXERCISE 4

The following outputs for the **Purchasing Managers** unit were considered. Three of them are "Outputs", mark them "O". Four are "Inputs", mark them "I". One is someone else's responsibility, mark it "S".

A   Supplier Relations
B   Inventory Level
C   Material Availability
D   Expediting
E   Materials Costs
F   Secondary Sources of Supply
G   Manufacturing Costs
H   Catalogue File Update

► ANSWER SHEETS

1 SALES MANAGER

A	Customer Relations	**I**
B	Sales Costs	**O**
C	Sales Levels	**O**
D	Product Line Profitability	**S**
E	New Customers	**O**
F	New Product Development	**S**
G	Advertising Policy	**S**
H	Sales Force Motivation	**I**

2 ACCOUNTANT

A	Management Information	**O**
B	Cost of Capital	**O**
C	Taxes	**O**
D	Cash Flows	**O**
E	Signing Cheques	**I**
F	Profit	**S**

3 PLANT MANAGER

A	New Customers	**S**
B	Manufacturing Cost	**O**
C	New Products	**S**
D	Quality	**O**
E	Plant Utilisation	**O**
F	Machine Maintenance	**I**
G	Hiring Employees	**I**

4 PURCHASING MANAGER

A	Supplier Relations	**I**
B	Inventory Level	**O**
C	Material Availability	**O**
D	Expediting	**I**
E	Materials Costs	**O**
F	Secondary Sources of Supply	**I**
G	Manufacturing Costs	**S**
H	Catalogue File Update	**I**

FEEDBACK SKILLS QUESTIONNAIRE

Use the following questionnaire to "test" your skills in giving feedback.

HELPFUL HINTS

- Here is an opportunity for you to upgrade your existing skill levels in the area of giving feedback.

- You can either complete this questionnaire on yourself or have it completed by people who work for you

- The results should help you to focus on any areas where there may be a skills gap, e.g. listening skills, active listening behaviours, or giving feedback.

Learning Skills	Never	Seldom	Occas-ionally	Frequently	Always
1 I listen for feelings, attitudes and perceptions, as well as for facts					
2 I try to listen for what is not said					
3 I avoid interrupting the person who is speaking					
4 I actually pay attention to who is speaking as opposed to "faking" attention					
5 I refrain from "tuning people out" because I don't like them, disagree with them, find them dull, etc.					
6 I work hard to avoid being distracted from what is said by the speaker's status, style, mannerisms, clothing, voice quality, voice pace, etc.					

Learning Skills (contd.)	Never	Seldom	Occas-ionally	Frequently	Always
7 I try to read the "nonverbals" — inflections, gestures, mood, posture, eye contact, facial expression, etc.					
8 I work hard at overcoming distractions (sounds, noises, movement, outside scenes, etc.) that may interfere with good listening					
9 I use non-verbal communication (eye contact, smiles, occasional head nods, etc.) to indicate that I wish to hear more					
10 I tend to restate or rephrase the other person's statements so that they will know that I have understood their point					
11 If I have not understood, I candidly admit this and ask for a restatement					
12 I avoid framing my response while the other person is still speaking					

Active Listening Behaviours

	Never	Seldom	Occas-ionally	Frequently	Always
13 I use "body language" to communicate interest					
14 I use encouraging words and phrases ("I see," "Uh huh," "Yes," etc.) to encourage free flow of conversation					
15 I maintain eye contact much of the time					
16 I use open-ended questions to encourage the other person to expand fully on their feelings					

	Never	Seldom	Occas-ionally	Frequently	Always
17 I listen quietly, and don't interrupt					
18 I use restatement to encourage communication					
19 I summarise at various points in the conversation					

Giving Feedback to Reviewees

20 I give employees feedback about their performance					
21 I give employees negative feedback although they don't like this					
22 I try not to compare the employee with other employees					
23 I give employees praise, even though they are embarrassed by it					
24 I criticise the action or behaviour, not the person					
25 I avoid giving criticism on more than one item					
26 I take account of the employee's sensitivity or receptivity to feedback					
27 I give feedback immediately after the incident occurs					
28 I don't give feedback when I am angry or upset					
29 I avoid sarcasm when giving feedback					
30 After I give feedback, I check for understanding					

	Never	Seldom	Occas-ionally	Frequently	Always
31 I avoid interrupting my employees while they are responding to my feedback					
32 I feel it is equally important to receive feedback as to give it					
33 I like to give feedback both orally and in writing					

SCORING THE QUESTIONNAIRE

The above questions are designed to stimulate your thinking about the process of giving feedback to others. If you discuss the questionnaire with people with whom you interact, you will have a better idea about the topic in general and your own needs for improvement in particular.

Score: Each of the above five ratings is allocated a score as follows:

Never   =   1
Seldom   =   2
Occasionally   =   3
Frequently   =   4
Always   =   5

149 – 165
Your understanding of, and skill in giving, feedback is excellent.

116 – 148
You have an above-average ability to give feedback. Further training will increase an already good skills set.

83 – 115
You have an average ability to give feedback.

50 – 82
You only have a fair ability to give feedback and definitely need to work on your skills in this area.

33 – 49

You are in very deep water. You need to develop some new skills before you go back in.

In Appendices F–L that follow, you are presented with seven case studies. These cases will test your understanding of the material covered in this book. They are based on real-life situations; each one presents you with a particular performance issue and challenges you to decide on how you would deal with it. They give you an opportunity to practise your analytical skills on providing interim coaching and feedback.

UNPUNCTUAL TYPIST

Mary Philips is the most reliable typist in your office. For the fifth time in the month you have seen her arriving over ten minutes late in the morning.

When you commented on her time-keeping last week, she apologised and referred to the unreliable bus service on her route. She said that the 8:13 bus often leaves early. If she misses it, there is no other bus until 8:35, which is too late. Last week Mary promised to make sure to be on time in future.

You are not sure whether to give Mary a real "ticking off", since good typists are hard to get nowadays.

What approach should you adopt?

THE CASE OF JACK PHILIPS

▶ I TAKE FULL RESPONSIBILITY

Jack Philips is the best worker in your team at Barco Batteries Ltd. For the third time in a month, you have found him working without protective gloves.

You "haul him over the coals", pointing out that he could be dismissed for the offence. He replies, "I know you warned me before and I know it's for my own good, sure, I could get a nasty acid burn. Still, a fellow gets absorbed in his work. Every so often I get sick and tired of those darn clumsy gloves. I don't know how anyone can expect us to do proper work when we're wearing them — and anyway if anything happens to me I will take full responsibility myself. So don't you worry about it anymore."

How would you deal with Jack?

THE CASE OF JOE SMITH

 UNDER THE WEATHER

You are in charge of the night shift in a factory. You notice that Joe Smith, an operative with an excellent record and 12 years' service appears to be missing from the five-man team in which he normally works. When you enquire where Smith is, Frank Reilly, a reliable older member of the team, takes you aside and explains that Smith came on duty "a bit under the weather" and Reilly persuaded him to remain in the men's room. Reilly pleads with you not to report Smith, saying that the remaining members of the group will keep the job going smoothly by foregoing their own breaks. The company policy is that drunkenness on duty will not be tolerated — another man was sacked for this offence only last month.

You interview Smith who claims to be "perfectly all right". He says he doesn't know what all the fuss is about. In your opinion, he is unfit for work.

What would you do?

I

THE CASE OF JOAN MYRES

▶ **MYRES DISCIPLINARY**

Joan Myres is now in trouble; up to the present she has had a tolerable work record as an accounts clerk. Recently she has made two minor errors in her work and these were overlooked by her supervisor. Today, she made a major error in making an unauthorised payment to a supplier who had provided a poor service; so poor was the service that management had decided not to pay the charge at all. Despite this she went ahead and paid the supplier. The payment could not be stopped because the cheque had been cashed immediately by the supplier. The managing director is enraged by the incident.

As Joan Myres' supervisor, please assess the case and **decide on a course of action**.

REBECCA GOES FOR GOLD

Rebecca Connolly is the Projects Manager. She has an honours B.Comm and a Master's Degree in Information Technology. She has been with the company for the past ten years, and was promoted to her current position two years ago. Rebecca's performance has historically been good and she has been responding well to her recently increased responsibilities.

The IT plans for the company have been unanimously agreed by the board. In the first three months of the review period, Rebecca has been responsible for the successful launch of two systems introductions ahead of schedule.

In terms of performance, the IT department is on target to exceed its goals at the mid-year review point.

Rebecca has introduced regular meetings with her subordinates to review progress on projects, and also to "brainstorm" additional IT opportunities to support the marketing area. Overall, employees in her department are highly motivated although she seems reluctant to identify training needs with regard to a small number of employees who she feels are performing below par.

What is your objective in meeting with Rebecca?

K

Eddie Johnson has been with the company for four years. As an Accounts Clerk he is responsible for several duties, many involving checking of calculations and processing reports. One of his most important duties is the matching of purchase orders with invoices received. The duty is important because invoices received and approved by Eddie involve considerable expense to be paid by the company.

In his four years with the company Eddie has always been conscientious and is generally accurate (in verifying calculations, matching invoices against purchase orders and ensuring full receipt of merchandise). While not a "world beater" he is steady and reliable. However, until recently, he has had trouble in keeping paperwork up to date. Some invoices were approved for payment several weeks after having been received which meant that payment on them was delayed. This resulted in suppliers' complaints to the finance department and then to you as Eddie's supervisor.

Lately, you have received very few complaints from auditing on invoices requiring adjustment. Invoices processed by Eddie are being processed accurately and quickly.

What outcome do you wish from your meeting with Eddie?

THE CASE OF "DOODLING DONAL"

 PROMOTIONAL ASSISTANT

Donal O'Brien is a new employee who has completed four months with the company. He is a Promotional Assistant in the marketing department and generally helps to co-ordinate the production and distribution of promotional materials for a range of financial products.

One of his specific duties is ensuring the delivery of product brochures to sales representatives.

The duty is somewhat complicated as it involves:

• Calculating the exact amount of brochures necessary to promote the constantly developing product range. Incorrect calculations can cause extensive wastage.

• Ordering the right quantities of brochures from many different printers and getting them to the reps.

• Scheduling production of the brochures and arranging their delivery exactly when product promotions will be held.

You have recently finished Donal's initial training programme. This covered an overview of his duties combined with some on-the-job practice given by an employee who held Donal's position prior to being promoted to a more senior one.

For the last two months Donal has been working on his own. In that time you have received several complaints from the senior sales reps about delays in receipt of brochures.

Also, you have just received a letter from a printing house requesting approval to dispose of a particularly expensive brochure for an old product which was ordered by mistake. You estimate the wastage to be in excess of £7,000.

Because of this wastage and the complaint you decide to talk to Donal about the two incidents. The events surprise you because Donal seemed to be well-trained, enthusiastic about his job and accurate during the on-the-job training period.

How tough or lenient should the company be with Donal?

SELF-ASSESSMENT OF TRAINING AND DEVELOPMENT NEEDS

Use this format to help your people "self-assess" their current skill levels.

 **MARKETING EXAMPLE**[1]

Memo to selected staff

One of my key job requirements is to identify additional training/development needs for our marketing group to help us continually improve our performance.

The attached Questionnaire has been designed to help you identify areas in which you may need further training and development. Please use additional sheets if required.

It is not a test. Please make an honest appraisal of yourself as this will allow us to develop realistic training programmes. We can meet on Tuesday next to discuss in more detail.

If you have any questions on the above please give me a call.

Best regards,

Amie Sheehan
Enc.

---

1 This would be typed in the standard memo format used within each company.

Preliminary Questionnaire

Assessment of Training/Development Needs for Marketing Personnel

1 My product knowledge on (list the products you personally handle) is:

Lacking in Depth   Expert

| 1 | 2 | 3 | 4 | 5 | 6 | 7 |

2 If you feel that your current product knowledge is less than adequate, how could this be strengthened?

_____

_____

_____

3 My knowledge of the marketplace environment for (same group) is:

Lacking in Depth   Expert

| 1 | 2 | 3 | 4 | 5 | 6 | 7 |

4 If your current knowledge of the marketplace is less than adequate, how could this be strengthened?

_____

_____

_____

5 My understanding of the underlying principles needed to market successfully (same group product) is:

Lacking in Depth   Expert

| 1 | 2 | 3 | 4 | 5 | 6 | 7 |

6 If your current knowledge of marketing principles is less than adequate, how could this be strengthened?

_____

_____

_____

7 How would you rate your ability to:

(a) Influence your peer group/manager to support your ideas.

To a small extent					To a great extent	
1	2	3	4	5	6	7

(b) Present your ideas coherently/persuasively.

To a small extent					To a great extent	
1	2	3	4	5	6	7

(c) Draw others/listen to/surface alternative ideas to your own.

To a small extent					To a great extent	
1	2	3	4	5	6	7

(d) Argue your position against a majority of dissenters.

To a small extent					To a great extent	
1	2	3	4	5	6	7

8 What actions do you intend to take in the next 12 months to strengthen your marketing knowledge or personal skills?

_____

_____

_____

9 What further training/development could the company provide to support your own effort in these areas?

_____

_____

_____

10 Any other comments you wish to make?

_____

_____

_____

Name _____   Date _____

Use this longer format to help your people diagnose their current skills levels/potential "gaps".

 MANAGERIAL PERSONNEL SAMPLE

Before completing this survey, please indicate your position, region and your function by placing an X in the appropriate box:

Position Category	General Manager	Executive Team	Country Management Team
Region	Europe	Japan	Latin America
Function	General Management	Marketing	Sales
	Finance	Manufacturing	Human Resources
	Medical	Legal	

Listed on the following pages are 47 competencies, i.e. knowledge, skills and abilities, divided into five categories, i.e. business management; people management; external/internal customer service; communications; career and personal development, that you may require in order to be fully proficient in your job.

To complete the Survey, please review each competency and indicate:

(a) How important it is for the job you are in (regardless of who fills it)

and

(b) How interested you are in improving your competence at the present time.

Thank you for your co-operation. Please return it to [named internal consultant or external organisation].

Circle one number in Column **a** and one number in Column **b** using the following scale:

1 = Extremely 2 = Very 3 = Quite 4 = Somewhat 5 = Hardly

Business Management	**a** How important is this competency for your current job?	**b** How interested are you in improving this competence?
1 Developing and communicating to others a "vision" for the organisation	1 2 3 4 5	1 2 3 4 5
2 Implementing your unit's strategic business plan	1 2 3 4 5	1 2 3 4 5
3 Communicating company values	1 2 3 4 5	1 2 3 4 5
4 Understanding economic, business, political and social trends and applying them to the business	1 2 3 4 5	1 2 3 4 5
5 Developing and implementing business plans and competitive strategies	1 2 3 4 5	1 2 3 4 5
6 Managing your unit as a business (financial analysis and control, budgeting, etc.)	1 2 3 4 5	1 2 3 4 5
7 Increased functional knowledge (own area)	1 2 3 4 5	1 2 3 4 5
8 Identifying and applying characteristics	1 2 3 4 5	1 2 3 4 5
9 Problem-solving and decision-making	1 2 3 4 5	1 2 3 4 5
10 Leading productive meetings	1 2 3 4 5	1 2 3 4 5
11 Project management	1 2 3 4 5	1 2 3 4 5
12 Completing tasks through those over whom you have no direct authority	1 2 3 4 5	1 2 3 4 5
13 Knowledge of business ethics	1 2 3 4 5	1 2 3 4 5

Business Management (contd.)	**a** How important is this competency for your current job?	**b** How interested are you in improving this competence?
14 Developing and communicating mission, values, organisational structure and products	1 2 3 4 5	1 2 3 4 5
15 Knowledge of administrative policies and procedures	1 2 3 4 5	1 2 3 4 5
16 Managing and utilising our technology	1 2 3 4 5	1 2 3 4 5
17 Utilising productivity and quality control techniques	1 2 3 4 5	1 2 3 4 5
18 Some other business management competency (what?)	1 2 3 4 5	1 2 3 4 5

People Management

19 Planning, organising, delegating and supervising work	1 2 3 4 5	1 2 3 4 5
20 Performance planning and appraisal	1 2 3 4 5	1 2 3 4 5
21 Team building	1 2 3 4 5	1 2 3 4 5
22 Participative management	1 2 3 4 5	1 2 3 4 5
23 Leading and motivating employees	1 2 3 4 5	1 2 3 4 5
24 Managing diversity	1 2 3 4 5	1 2 3 4 5
25 Coaching and counselling	1 2 3 4 5	1 2 3 4 5
26 Creating individual development plans	1 2 3 4 5	1 2 3 4 5
27 Interviewing and recruiting employees	1 2 3 4 5	1 2 3 4 5
28 Providing career counselling	1 2 3 4 5	1 2 3 4 5
29 Handling difficult personnel problems (substance abuse, sexual harassment)	1 2 3 4 5	1 2 3 4 5
30 Some other people-management competency (what?)	1 2 3 4 5	1 2 3 4 5

External/Internal Customer Service	**a** How important is this competency for your current job?	**b** How interested are you in improving this competence?
31 Building and maintaining customer relationships	1 2 3 4 5	1 2 3 4 5
32 Identifying customer needs and developing and implementing plans to satisfy those needs	1 2 3 4 5	1 2 3 4 5
33 Negotiating win-win agreements with customers	1 2 3 4 5	1 2 3 4 5
34 Some other customer service competency (what?)	1 2 3 4 5	1 2 3 4 5

Communications

35 Presentation skills	1 2 3 4 5	1 2 3 4 5
36 Effective writing	1 2 3 4 5	1 2 3 4 5
37 Interpersonal communications	1 2 3 4 5	1 2 3 4 5
38 Assertiveness and influencing skills	1 2 3 4 5	1 2 3 4 5
39 Listening skills	1 2 3 4 5	1 2 3 4 5
40 Reading skills	1 2 3 4 5	1 2 3 4 5
41 Editing and critiquing the written work of others	1 2 3 4 5	1 2 3 4 5
42 Some other communications competency (what?)	1 2 3 4 5	1 2 3 4 5

Career/Personal Development	**a** How important is this competency for your current job?	**b** How interested are you in improving this competence?
43 Managing your own career growth and development	1 2 3 4 5	1 2 3 4 5
44 Time management	1 2 3 4 5	1 2 3 4 5
45 Stress management	1 2 3 4 5	1 2 3 4 5
46 Balancing your professional and personal life	1 2 3 4 5	1 2 3 4 5
47 Some other competency (what?)	1 2 3 4 5	1 2 3 4 5

THE DOUG MEYER CASE:
FACILITATOR'S NOTES

CASE SUMMARY

The case is primarily designed to create discussion around the "degrees of freedom" which any manager has on joining a new team. The case specifically focuses on the business impact of a managerial change in Sterling Winthrop, when Doug Meyer joined the company as President of the North American Division in October 1991. The hope is that lessons learned from an in-depth understanding of success in this particular case may be more easily replicated and perpetuated elsewhere.

EFFECTIVE LEADERSHIP

There are several components of this particular case. Firstly, it is, primarily a story of effective leadership. It details the process where positive change is consciously designed and shows the skill of visioning, the mapping of bold business frontiers and eliciting support for this.

MANAGERIAL ROLE MODELLING

Secondly, the case is aimed at helping managers understand the impact of role modelling — the critical influence of behaviour in shaping the perceptions and attitudes of others. The use of a planned "entry strategy" to strengthen this overtly is a particular feature of note in this case.

MANAGING CHANGE

Finally, the case offers several valuable lessons about managing change. It provides a context for discussing the tensions associated with major business transformations and details several sub-possibilities under this critical heading.

 TEACHING METHOD AND MATERIALS

An open discussion with the entire class is recommended as the major method. This will capitalise on the collective information and thinking of the group and generate the richest discussion. The questions set out below will be useful in working with the class.

KEY QUESTIONS IN FACILITATING THE GROUP

- What type of climate existed at the Sterling Winthrop USA Division prior to Meyer's arrival? Why was this the case?

- What were the "givens", e.g. the primary causes of the decline in business performance and the strengths of the business Meyer inherited?

- From an organisation perspective, how do you manage people who are unsuccessful in seeking an internal promotion?

- How do you respond to the notion of a consciously designed "entry strategy"? In your opinion, was Doug Meyer's strategy correct for the particular circumstances? Would you have adopted a different stance?

- What were the key "events" which Doug Meyer orchestrated in his early days? What was the impact of these? What other options existed?

- Doug Meyer deviated from his initial "softly, gently" approach at a fairly early point. In hindsight, was this the correct route? Faced with similar circumstances what do you think you would have done?

- Are there key differences between a manager and leader? What are these differences? How would you describe Doug Meyer?

- How important is the personal leadership exercised by a single individual in any business turnaround programme? Would it have happened anyway?

▶ PREPARATION QUESTIONS TO GO WITH THE CASE MATERIAL

Participants should read the case before coming to class and be prepared to deal with four key questions (which can be distributed with the case material).

1 What was the initial "entry strategy" chosen by Doug Meyer? How would you evaluate this?

2 What was the initial impact of Meyer on the existing group in Sterling Winthrop, USA? What influenced this perception?

3 What are the lessons for any new manager in developing an "entry strategy" for a new position?

4 How important is the personal leadership exercised by a single individual in any business turnaround programme?

▶ TEACHING SCHEDULE

- Introduction to the case, overview of the issues and description of the schedule — 10 minutes.

- Sub-group discussion to address the four pre-class assignment questions and the additional key questions provided by the facilitator (it is advised that no more than four teams be created) — 45 minutes to 1 hour.

- The teams should present their ideas to the total group in 15-20 minute presentations. Presentations and discussion – 1½ hours.

▶ SUPPLEMENTAL READINGS

The "I" of the Hurricane
Art McNeil, Pelanduk Pub., Malaysia, 1990

The Making of an Achiever
Allan Cox, Dood, Mead. New York, 1984

Leadership is an Art
Max De Pree, Doubleday, New York, 1989

EMPLOYEE TEAMS:
FACILITATOR'S NOTES

CASE SUMMARY

This case traces the evolution of the Employee Participation Program at the McPherson Plant in Kansas. The key focus is on the timeframe 1986 through 1992. It documents the transformation from an employee participation ideal into a fully fledged working system — a manufacturing plant of empowered employees.

The development of the Employee Involvement Teams and the description of the processes associated with them provide a rich basis for a class discussion. There are several components of the McPherson plant story.

ESTABLISHING PLANT AUTONOMY

Firstly, it is aimed at describing the success of a sub-unit within a large company; an understanding of this particular success may make it possible for managers in other multinational subsidaries to establish their "degress of freedom".

EFFECTIVE LEADERSHIP

Secondly, it is a story of effective leadership. The difficulty of cultural change within organisations and the timeframes needed to accomplish this are clearly detailed. It highlights the fact that leadership (defined as the ability to create positive change) is not solely a

CEO function, but an expectation from all leaders, regardless of level within an organisation. Ultimately, it describes a new school of leadership which allows an organisation to achieve its vision through the empowerment of its people.

MANAGING CHANGE

There are also valuable lessons about managing change to be learned from this case. It provides a context for discussing the tensions associated with transformations — is it best achieved through evolution or revolution, are incremental or quantum steps most likely to succeed, should it be planned on a companywide or on a small "seeding" basis? The case provides a salutary lesson; people normally don't resist change, they resist being changed.

 KEY QUESTIONS IN FACILITATING THE GROUP

The case raises a number of crucial questions about the development of an Employee Participation Program. The following questions will be useful in working with the class:

- What was the underlying reason for the change? Did a particular vision exist which initially drove the empowerment theme? Where had this come from?

- Why did the earlier Quality Circles initiative fail?

- How were the changes planned? Was this a successful strategy?

- How do you deal with people who were successful

under a different regime but find it difficult to cope in a new environment?

- How important is the personal leadership exercised by a single individual in any change programme? Was Tom Berry's role particularly influential or were the Employee Involvement Teams something which would have evolved anyway?

- How much autonomy should local plants exercise? How should they respond if there is conflict with a local idea versus a view taken by a corporate staff group?

- How important is the general management/ employee relationship to the success of a participative structure? What assumptions could you infer about the general climate at the plant?

- What is the likely next stage of development?

▶ TEACHING METHOD AND MATERIALS

This case can be taught several different ways. An open discussion with the entire class is recommended as the major method. This will capitalise on the collective information and thinking of the group and generate the richest discussion. Participants should read the case before coming to class and be prepared to deal with the following four key questions (which can be distributed with the case material).

▶ PREPARATION QUESTIONS TO GO WITH THE CASE MATERIAL:

1 Why did the Employee Involvement Teams system evolve at McPherson?

2 Why is the current system deemed successful? What are the benefits/potential downsides?

3 What can be learned from the case about managing change? Are there ways in which it could have been managed more successfully?

4 What do you recommend should be done to foster the growth and development of empowerment within your organisation? What can you personally do to support this?

 ## TEACHING SCHEDULE

- Introduction to the case, overview of the issues and description of the schedule — 10 minutes.

- Sub-group discussion to address the four pre-class assignment questions and the additional key questions provided by the facilitator (it is advised that no more than four teams be created) — 45 minutes to 1 hour.

- The teams should present their ideas to the group in 15-20 minute presentations. Presentations and discussion — 1½ hours.

 ## SUPPLEMENTAL READINGS

The Transformation of American Industrial Relations, Basic Books, New York 1986.

"By Days I Make The Cars", *Harvard Business Review* pp 106/115. Vol. 58, No. 3 May/June 1990

"Do Supervisors Thrive In Participative Work Systems?", *Organizational Dynamics*, USA, Winter 1979

BIBLIOGRAPHY

Patricia Aburdene and John Naisbitt, *Reinventing the Corporation* (Warner Books Inc, New York, 1985).

Karl Albrecht and Ron Zemke, *Service America* (Dow Jones-Irwin, New York, 1985).

William Band, *Creating Value for Customers: Designing and Implementing a Total Corporate Strategy* (Wiley, London, 1991).

Clutterbuck and Goldsmith, *The Winning Streak* (Penguin Books, London, 1985).

Deal and Kennedy, *Corporate Cultures: The Rights and Rituals of Corporate Life* (Addison Wesley, Reading (Mass), 1982).

Edward Demming, *Out of the Crisis* (MIT Press, Cambridge (Mass), 1986).

Peter Drucker, *The Effective Executive* (Pan Books, London, 1970).

Robert Fulmer, Professor of Organisation Development, College of William & Mary, USA, conversation with the author.

El Namaki MSS, "Creating a Corporate Vision" (*Long Range Planning*, Vol 25 No. 6, pp 25–29, UK, 1992).

John Hynes (now General Manager of An Post, speaking to the IPD Conference, Killarney, 1994).

Klemm et al, *Values-Based Leadership* (HRP's 1993 Annual Conference Paper, USA).

Rosabeth Moss-Kanter, *The Change Masters* (Allen and Unwin, London, 1983).

Gene Perret, *Funny Business* (Prentice-Hall, New Jersey, USA, 1990).

Tom Peters, *Thriving on Chaos: The Handbook for Management Revolution* (Alfred A. Knopf, New York, 1987).

Tom Peters and Robert Waterman, *In Search of Excellence* (Harper and Row, New York, 1982).

Bill Reddin, *The Output-Oriented Organisation* (Gower Publishing, London, 1988).

Mike Robinson, *The Journey to Excellence* (Wiley, Chichester, 1986).

Buck Rodgers, *The IBM Way: Insights into the World's Most Successful Organisation* (Harper and Row, New York, 1986).

Maurice Sains (Professor of Organisational Behaviour, Insead, France, speaking at a Management Development Programme with Sterling Winthrop, 1992).

Isadore Sharpe, *(Fortune*, March 1989).

Robert Waterman, *The Frontiers of Excellence* (Nicholas Brearley Publishing, London, 1994).

Tom Watson Snr (former Chairman of IBM). (Quoted by Arthur Young Consulting Group — *Strategic Planning for the large firm*, New York, 1992).

David Whitwam, "The Right Way to go Global" (*Harvard Business Review*, Mar/April 1994).